X̄

SPIRITUAL FATHERS

The Way Forward

Guiding Younger Men in a Changing Culture

MAN IN THE MIRROR

maninthemirror.org

X̄

SPIRITUAL FATHERS

The idea of spiritual fathers long precedes this study and this movement. Our hope is that you take your position in restoring the lineage of courageous men who have fathered and discipled other men since the beginning of time.

As we continue to press forth with our goal of empowering 10,000 spiritual fathers, we can't wait to see how God uses you to guide younger men toward the Way, the Truth, and the Life.

It's a worthy calling.

TABLE OF CONTENTS

INTRODUCTION

Start Here—But Don't Start Alone

Welcome to a significant and practical learning journey! This study was written for you to better understand what is happening in the spiritual life of young men today. Engaging a younger man in a meaningful relationship will not only change his life and yours, but it will build the Kingdom of God. You have the potential to make a tremendous impact on another man that will ripple through his key relationships, marriage, family, church, and workplace.

A men's small group is a perfect way to process this material. If you picked up this book on your own, we encourage you to invite a couple other men to join you on this learning journey to process and pray together.

Meeting Weekly with Your Small Group

Plan on devoting about two hours each week to prep and meet time:

1. Read one chapter per week in this small group study guide. You can read the chapter separately ahead of time, jotting down notes for discussion in the group, or read the chapter together as part of your group time, alternating readers section by section. Allow an extra 20-30 minutes of meeting time if you choose the second option.

2. Use the Discussion Questions at the end of each chapter to foster a deeper discussion.

3. Reserve the last 15-20 minutes to share prayer requests and pray for each other. Each chapter includes a prayer guide at the end with space for notes.

Spiritual Son Considerations

Over the next 12 weeks, it is our prayer that you learn a lot about what's happening with younger men and seriously consider the option of engaging a younger man as you finish this study. You may already have a potential spiritual son in mind, or you might have several possibilities in mind to share with your group and pray about together. Take your time. You don't have to make a commitment today but keep your mind and heart open to what God might say to you about your investment as a Spiritual Father in the future.

For now, use the space below to keep track of who you feel God might be leading you to as a Spiritual Father. You will discuss and pray over these names with your group.

Name	How do I know them?	Common Interests or Connections
1.		
2.		
3.		
4.		
5.		

SPIRITUAL FATHERING

CHAPTER 1

THE NEED FOR SPIRITUAL FATHERS

The church needs emotionally and spiritually healthy men—men of character who strive to be good husbands, fathers, and friends. Men who are aware of their flaws and want to repent and grow in Christ. Men who mature from "young men who have overcome the evil one" to being fathers who "know Him who is from the beginning" (see 1 John 2:12-14).

But something is missing.

Man in the Mirror has worked with thousands of churches, and a common refrain we hear is that it's difficult to draw or engage young men. The stories are legion of young men who grew up in the church, only to walk into adulthood and subsequently walk out of the church. This "de-churching" phenomenon should prompt some self-reflection by those of us in the church.

Many of the activities that used to appeal to a broad range of men aren't effectively reaching this demographic, such as large-group meetings, traditional Bible studies, or prayer breakfasts.

Indeed, in a recent survey conducted by Ryan Burge, respondents between the ages of 27-45 were asked why they left the church. The #1 reason given was that they didn't fit in.[1]

Furthermore, the survey revealed this striking statistic: When asked, "At which point in your life were you the most religious?" 70% of *all* young men—both de-churched *and* churched—indicated it was at least ten years prior to taking the survey.

So how do we answer the call to disciple the next generation of men (see Titus 2) if the next generation feels disconnected, detached, or disinterested? How do we bridge the gaps?

The Cultural Gap

These concerns aren't new. On the contrary, since at least the 1960s, the American church has feared losing the next generation. A lot of time, money, and energy has been dedicated to combating it through efforts like college ministry, events, and other youth initiatives.

---

[1]Ryan Burge, PhD, *The Dechurched Initiative*, 2022

While those efforts were noble and genuine, the fears fueling them weren't always valid. The research shows that throughout the 80s, 90s, and even into the early 2000s, the church was not falling into the abyss of irrelevancy. In fact, much of American culture was still faith-based, and many men were being reached with the gospel.

Even on a global level, the positive place of religion or faith was on the rise during this time. In the largest statistical study of religion in the world, researchers examined 49 countries—which comprised 60% of the world's population—and found that 33 of them were increasingly more religious, more focused on faith, and at the very least seeking God.[2]

> *Historically one of the most diverse and free places for faith, the U.S. is now the 12th least religious country in the world.*

But lately, the religious landscape—especially for men—has shifted, and the data is alarming. From 2007-2022, all expressions of religious faith are dramatically down in 42 of those same 49 countries. And in the U.S., historically one of the most diverse and free places for faith, we are now the 12th least religious country in the world.[3] In fact, today Christianity seems to be viewed *negatively* for the first time, as Christian moral views increasingly come into conflict with secular moral order.[4]

This goes far beyond the "culture wars." Young men today are gradually finding it irrelevant to seek answers in traditional places. Social media, podcasts, and other forms of technology offer a constant stream of opinions and worldviews to the point of mental exhaustion. Every view, lifestyle, and belief is valid.

As Sebastian in the 2016 movie La La Land (played by Ryan Gosling) quipped about the people around him: "They worship everything, and they value nothing." The postmodern chickens have come home to roost.

It is against this cultural backdrop that traditional forms of ministry are struggling to get through to men in their 20s and 30s. Simply inviting a young man to a church-based men's event is frequently unsuccessful. And instead of seeing a traditional Bible study as a place for honest questions and trustworthy answers, it's more likely to be viewed as just one of many readily available worldviews and systems—or worse, as a place with tired, irrelevant answers from the past.

Relationally, they seem to be more connected to their peers than ever. However, although they may be able to efficiently monitor the lives of their friends around the world through social media, they rarely experience the fellowship of a backyard BBQ. They can connect immediately with just about anyone, but those interactions

---

[2]Ronald F. Inglehart, Religion's Sudden Decline: *What's Causing it, and What Comes Next?* (Oxford, 2021), p. 1.
[3]Ibid.
[4]https://www.firstthings.com/article/2022/02/the-three-worlds-of-evangelicalism, (accessed 7/26/22)

are often stilted, reduced to short sentences and emojis. Face-to-face human interactions and real conversations can be rare.

They use GPS to locate their children, websites to track their schoolwork, and apps to order anything from groceries to furniture that gets delivered right to their door. They can stream shows and movies and sports. The answer to any question is just a few keystrokes away.

> *There has never been a generation of men with* more *resources and* less *nurturing.*

In contrast, you may have grown up writing letters, watching the nightly news, reading newspapers, and doing everything face-to-face. You received your information from a few trusted sources, while today younger men can get information from hundreds or even thousands of sources—few of them trustworthy.

From one perspective, they have the world at their fingertips. But although it may fuel the *feeling* of intimacy with others, the connections are often superficial and short-lived.

For many of the men we hear from, a deep loneliness persists. In a very real sense, there has never been a generation of men with *more* resources and *less* nurturing.

As the book *Dopamine Nation* points out, we have a generation of men whose brains have been rewired from a constant stream of stimuli, dopamine rushes, and distractions.[5] And by using social media to share only the most attractive moments of our lives, we can, in effect, hide in plain sight.

The Fatherhood Gap

In addition to being starved for real human connection, men are increasingly less likely to have had a father who was or is physically present—and the percentage continues to shrink.

In 2021, according to the U.S. Census Bureau, 18.4 million children—1 in 4—lived without a biological, step, or adoptive father in the home.[6]

Furthermore, some fathers who were *physically* present weren't *emotionally* present.

These father wounds can be deep and long-lasting, and as young men begin building families of their own, it creates a compounding effect. One man, Craig, recalled feeling crushed by the weight of it:

---

[5]Anna Lembke, MD, *Dopamine Nation: Finding Balance in the Age of Indulgence* (Dutton, 2021).
[6]U.S. Census Bureau. (2021). Living arrangements of children under 18 years old: 1960 to present. Washington, D.C.: U.S. Census Bureau.

I'd met Kristy, a believer, and we married when I was just 21 years old. My dad had been absent a lot when I was growing up, and although I loved Kristy, it quickly became apparent that I had no idea how to be a man for her or how to die to myself.

We had five kids within 10 years, and I was gone a lot for work. When I was home with my family, I felt angry and out of control, stemming from my frustration from not knowing how to be a husband or how to be a father. I'd been set up to fail, and that's what I was doing.

At Man in the Mirror, we say, "No man fails on purpose." And it's true. Men like Craig want to succeed; but it's extremely difficult with no guide to follow. Some manage to make do and figure out life through trial and error. Others experience enormous pressure to numb the pain through distraction, addiction or other sinful behavior, and the collateral damage is staggering.

Steve, another man who shared his story with our ministry, had a very different experience than Craig. Consider the impact of a father who was not only physically and emotionally present, but *spiritually* present as well:

My father was my hero, confidante, spiritual father, and mentor. Any time I was lonely, depressed, sick, or fearful, my father was just a phone call away. Somehow, he just had a way of encouraging me and praying with me that always made me feel better. Also, when I felt spiritually inspired by the things that God was revealing to me from His word, Dad was the one that I would go to. He was a spiritual giant.

But things changed quickly when my dad and I both contracted Covid-19. I survived it. He did not.

I loved my father, and believe I was the most privileged man in the world. Dad was a pianist and organist in his church who inspired me musically and made me want to make the teaching of music to young students my lifelong passion and career.

I was able to tell him many times how much I loved and honored him, and that the man I am today was due to the way he loved me, prayed for me, taught me, inspired me, and encouraged me my whole life.

Since his passing, I have been determined to follow in his footsteps. I couldn't think of a better way to do that than to join the same weekly small group of men that my dad was a part of and invested in for several years.

Since I started attending these weekly Bible study and prayer meetings, I cannot tell you how much joy and comfort I gain when I am with them. I would never miss a week, because I need other like-minded, Spirit-filled men in order to continue growing in Christ.

We were not put here on this earth in this space and time just to exist. We all have something to do. Jesus said, "The harvest is plentiful, but the laborers are few." I want to be a man who is willing to get out of his comfort zone, spiritually lead, and make a difference in our world. (And I believe I am with other men like that right now!)

> *It can feel intimidating to consider bridging the fatherhood gap for a younger man. You can overcome that apprehension through training, tools, prayer, and supportive community.*

In his dad, Steve saw a life worth imitating—so much so that he sought out the same paths his father had walked. But just as the presence of his father instilled in him a desire to pursue a formal discipleship group with older men, the opposite can be equally true.

We believe the *lack* of present fathers is a factor that often undermines the appeal of traditional men's ministry efforts in the lives of young men. In many ways, it's a problem of trust. Fatherless young men may desire a meaningful relationship with a father figure who will guide them, but they have yet to experience a positive relationship with a more mature man.

Because of this, an invitation to a group event, retreat, or class with older men can feel unfamiliar and uncomfortable, or even be met with suspicion.

Of course, older men also have wounds when it comes to father-son relationships. Most never had what Steve had. Perhaps your own father was absent, distant, or worse.

As a result, it can feel intimidating to consider bridging the fatherhood gap for a younger man. But we want to help you overcome that apprehension through training, tools, prayer, and a supportive community.

The Discipleship Gap

Thankfully, there are plenty of biblical churches in the U.S., led by leaders whose faith and passion are genuine. They're committed to good things, such as evangelism, missions, outreach, and solid preaching. Yes, the soil for ministry may be harder and more brittle, but men are still being reached for Christ.

But we face a discipleship gap in the church today. As many as 40% of Christians do nothing to grow spiritually outside of Sunday worship. Only 28% of Christians say they are engaged in any type of discipleship. And a meager 5% report that they meet with an older Christian one-on-one.[7]

> **Only 28% of Christians say they are engaged in any type of discipleship.**

The impact is profound. Of the Christians who are not engaged in discipleship, just 30% say their relationship with Jesus brings them deep joy and satisfaction.[8]

When asked their opinion of a simple statement—"my faith in Jesus impacts the way I live my life every day"—65% of those in a discipleship community agreed, while only 26% of those who aren't engaged in discipleship agreed.[9]

Having a discipleship relationship, such as a mentor or spiritual father figure, is critical. Without it, we're on life support with a faith that is weaker, thinner, and more prone to fail when tested.

The fact is, because of this gap, young men who love Christ are experiencing much of the same confusion as the world around them. We have both the opportunity and responsibility to meet this challenge.

Bridging the cultural gap, the fatherhood gap, and the discipleship gap is what spiritual fathering is all about.

A Way Forward: Spiritual Fathers

A new approach is needed to reach younger men for Christ. The younger men we've interacted with have consistently expressed interest in a real relationship with an older man of character who can guide them. The demand is there.

> **Bridging the cultural gap, the fatherhood gap, and the discipleship gap is what spiritual fathering is all about.**

But there is also clear evidence that older men—like you—want these relationships. In the same study on discipleship, *83% of older men said they would love to disciple a younger man, but they need help to feel qualified and equipped.*[10]

If you have a heart for younger men and for Christ, you're already qualified. And we are determined to fully equip you to develop meaningful relationships that will change lives and build the kingdom of God.

To become a spiritual father is to, over time, develop a deep, intentional spiritual friendship with a younger man. As you walk through life together, our prayer is that,

---

[7]https://www.barna.com/research/christians-discipleship-community/ (accessed 7/1/22)
[8]Ibid.
[9]Ibid.
[10]Ibid., emphasis added

eventually, he will be prepared to become a spiritual father to a man behind him on the journey as well.

In the next chapter, we will further define and explore your role as a spiritual father. But first, take time to review some key takeaways and discuss what you've read with another person or group.

> *If you have a heart for younger men and for Christ, you're already qualified.*

Takeaways

- Studies showed interest in Christian faith growing worldwide prior to 2007, but then waning in the years since.

- Just over 1 in 4 Christians in church are engaged in discipleship, and 1 in 20 are engaged one-on-one with a mentor or older Christian.

- Younger men are suffering from a lack of fathering.

- Younger men are hyperconnected by technology; yet their relationships are superficial, and their belief in truth is undermined.

- Many younger men are expressing a desire for a spiritual father.

- While many mature Christian men understand the need to be discipling someone else, they often feel unequipped and unqualified.

Discussion Questions

1) What do you think young men need the most today?

2) When you hear the term "spiritual father," how does that make you feel (e.g., eager, anxious, sad, hopeful, etc.)? Why?

3) Have you ever had a spiritual father? Who? How did they help you? If not, do you wish you had?

4) Have you ever served as a spiritual father (mentor, spiritual coach, guide)? What were some highs and lows of that experience?

Prayer

Take a few minutes and share prayer requests around the group in the following areas: family, work, social, and personal. Share any concerns you have about becoming a spiritual father.

Notes

CHAPTER 2

YOUR ROLE AS A SPIRITUAL FATHER

Many of the men answering the call to be spiritual fathers have been in church a long time. Over the years, it can become rarer and rarer to hear a sermon you've never heard before. Months or even years may pass before a book on Christian living, or a small group study provides brand-new insight.

Here's the potential problem: if you define discipleship only as things you can learn intellectually, you're done. Spiritually retired.

So how do you grow if you've already acquired 95% of the knowledge you're ever going to?

Start giving yourself away. You start hanging out with men who think differently than you do and who have different experiences and perspectives—men who need what you have to offer, *and vice versa.*

The relationship between a spiritual father and son is one of mutual affection and growth. While younger men search for love and guidance from an experienced, trustworthy source, older men often hunger for new adventures and ways to be used by God. We hope to meet the needs and desires of both groups through connecting them in authentic friendships, while providing the relational skills, spiritual depth, and resources needed.

> *Engaging in your faith in new ways will energize and grow you more fully into who God created you to be—lacking nothing and equipped to disciple others.*

If you've never done something like this before, you're in the right place! Engaging your faith in new ways will energize and grow you more fully into who God created you to be—lacking in nothing and equipped to disciple others.

You are far from spiritually retired. Rather, you're newly hired—for one of the most important roles you'll ever take on.

The purpose in providing this guidebook is to provide you with effective strategies to listen and encourage younger men in their walk with Christ. We want you to be Paul to a younger Timothy—loving him, caring for him, and supporting him. We want you to be a voice of encouragement, and if needed, a voice of reason when he struggles with sin.

We hope you can see yourself as a spiritual father figure to one young man.

Envision an authentic relationship, not a group study, built on a sense of trust. Yes, you may be called to invest in two or more men, but if you invest in one, then you are a faithful steward of your calling.

A Note of Caution

Before we go further, we want to provide a note of caution on the term "spiritual fathers."

First, why "fathers"? Why did we not use "teachers" or "coaches" or even "mentors"?

We chose the word "fathers" because we want older men to make it clear to younger men that, without a doubt—

- They're going to care about them,
- They're going to walk alongside them in life,
- And they will pursue them even when they're hurting and it's messy—in fact, *especially* when they're hurting and it's messy.

The fact is there are too many spiritual orphans out there. And as the number increases, the church's love and concern for them should also increase, with mature disciples determined to meet them where they are, adopting them spiritually, and build relationships.

But the term "spiritual father" should only be used as *internal* language—i.e., with other men engaged in this spiritual fathering small group study.

This means you probably shouldn't approach a younger man and ask him if he wants to be your "spiritual son" or if he'd like a "spiritual father." To use this phrasing with a person you're hoping to serve—especially without context—will likely be foreign, jarring, or even off-putting.

> *Strong bonds are built through presence over time, shared experiences, and mutual Christian affection.*

Strong bonds are built through presence over time, shared experiences, and mutual Christian affection. With young men especially, if you violate the normal process of relationships by "coming in hot," it will likely damage the prospect of a close relationship eventually forming.

Mountain Guides: A Helpful Framework

When you think about the role of a spiritual father and what he has to offer, consider the role of a mountain guide.

Imagine that you decided to climb Mt. Everest. You've watched a documentary or two, and so you know that the first thing you need to do is hire a guide.

You talk to David from the First Everest Guide Service over the phone and arrange your expedition. After overcoming a lot of travel obstacles, you finally arrive at Base Camp—excited, nervous, and eager to get going.

David is there, all smiles, and greets you with a hearty handshake. "You ready to do this thing?" he asks enthusiastically. You take a deep breath and nod.

David reaches into his pack and pulls out a book for you: *How to Climb Mt. Everest: A Primer*. Then he hands you a folded-up map. You open it and see a picture of the mountain with a red line and several X's.

> *The biblical model we want to adopt for discipleship includes guiding and going with someone; it's Jesus' model when He said, "Come, follow me."*

"That's your route and those X's are base camps," David says. Then he hands you a gear list and points to a pile of equipment. You see air tanks, parkas, mittens, crampons, and ropes. "Grab whatever you need."

Finally, he puts his arm around your shoulders and turns you toward the mountain. It's a clear day and you can see the summit, snow billowing off it like smoke from a chimney on a windy day. "Amazing, isn't it?" David says. "Okay, go get 'em, Tiger!"

In dismay, you realize you're in huge trouble. While he may have given you most everything you need from an equipment and information standpoint, what you really need is for him to go *with* you.

Discipleship is the same way. We can read books and take notes on sermons, but we also desperately need someone to go with us. The biblical model we want to adopt for discipleship includes *guiding and going* with someone; it's Jesus' model when He said, "Come, follow me." This is the essence of spiritual fathering.

Your role as a spiritual father is to be a *guide* who:

- **Has been there before.** You wouldn't want to hire a guy to get you up Mt. Everest who has never been there before. You want someone who knows what it takes. They've stood on the summit, and even failed a few times before they got there.

- **Goes with you on the trip.** Climbing Mt. Everest is dangerous. There are ice falls, crevasses, blisteringly cold winds, unpredictable weather conditions, too little oxygen, and a lot of suffering. A good guide experiences every one of those difficulties and dangers alongside you.

- **Tells *and* shows.** A good mountain guide teaches you to do things for yourself by modeling it. He doesn't expect you to read about tying a knot or working an oxygen tank. He shows you how to do it and checks to make sure it's right, over and over, until he's confident you know how to do it. He even teaches you to check his work, so that you can protect each other.

All around you are young men looking at the mountain right now, wondering how it's even possible to climb toward the summit. What they most need is not an outwardly perfect guy with a perfect family, or a Bible scholar who seems brilliant.

They need someone whose face is leathery from the harsh conditions, who has lost a finger or two to frostbite, who has failed a few times but kept on trying for the summit, and whose love for Christ and others is obvious.

The struggles you've faced haven't disqualified you—quite the opposite. Younger men have strength and passion. What they are lacking is the experience and wisdom you've picked up along the way.

How has God provided for you to guide younger men as they are trying to solve the problems they feel? The answer is that the lessons you've learned are exactly the same lessons young men need.

4 Reminders from Paul to Help Guide You

In the Apostle Paul's writings, he often refers to Timothy as his "son." Here are four reminders from the opening verses of Paul's letter 2 Timothy that will help guide a spiritual father:

1. Remind yourself it's by the will of God.
Paul begins the letter of 2 Timothy with: "Paul, an apostle of Christ Jesus *by the will of God* according to the promise of the life that is in Christ Jesus" (1:1, emphasis added).

In effect, Paul says, "I didn't go find God. God came and found me." When you're discipling someone, it's not just about you. It's about the will of God. That's really good news! Because if it's by the will of God, then He'll make a way for it!

You might feel like you have no idea who needs a spiritual father or where to even begin. Look around. Pray that you'll sense the will of God as you do.

2. Remind him of who he is in Christ.
Paul opens his letter with that verse perhaps so that he can also remind Timothy of "the promise of life that is in Christ."

We, too, need to remind men of this—in a world that directs us toward so many other things, we find our identity and life in Jesus. "I am the way, the truth, and the life," Jesus said (see John 14:6).

We need to talk often about God's grace and the meaning of the gospel. Remind younger men that it's not about our performance; it's about Jesus' sacrifice.

If you get the opportunity to be a spiritual father to a younger man who does not yet know or trust Christ, your approach will be more nuanced, but it could be a remarkable experience for you both. As you gently guide him toward faith in Jesus, you may get the privilege of witnessing the remarkable process of a man being regenerated by the Holy Spirit and placing his trust in Christ for the first time!

3. Remind him of his gifts.

Paul saw something in Timothy when he met him, and he said, "I want this guy with me. I want to bring him along with me as I go." But he didn't just recognize his gifts; he reminded him to *use* them.

In 2 Timothy 1, Paul writes, "For this reason I remind you to fan into flame the gift of God, which is in you through the laying on of my hands, for God gave us a spirit not of fear but of power and love and self-control" (v. 6-7).

What happens when you don't use your talents and gifts? The same thing that happens to the flames when you don't feed a fire; they fade. As a spiritual father, as we identify gifts and talents, we need to encourage guys to use them out in the world to make a difference.

Paul ends his opening with a punch, essentially saying, "Timothy, don't be afraid. When you're afraid, Timothy, that's not the spirit of God. The spirit of God is a spirit of power and love and self-control. You can do this. You've got this. Why? Because the Holy Spirit is with you, my beloved child." Imagine how powerful that reminder was—and how powerful it still is today!

4. Remind him of the way God wants him to live.

This relates to biblical ethics—living a godly life. It's the way we work. It's the way we love our family. It's the way we spend time with God. It's the way we handle conflict. It's how we cope with hardships. It's the way we engage in our neighborhoods.

After establishing trust, a spiritual father can start talking to a man about where he is struggling the most, and then helping him apply biblical truth to those areas of his life. One at a time.

When he asks for advice, there's a great opportunity and privilege to remind him of how God wants us to live.

The Need for Soft Skills

The rest of this guidebook will take a different approach than most men's discipleship training.

In our experience, discipleship training tends to focus primarily on rules or biblical truths. Books routinely start with the problem—men need Christian truth for their lives—and they dive straight into training men in the Bible.

This is often set up as a series of rules to live by—sort of a "Seven Habits for Highly Effective Christians."

The problem, as discussed in the previous chapter, is that young men who may be short on real relationships are almost certainly short on real relationships with older men. For them, launching into a study or a set of rules to live by feels like they are being hit with an agenda.

The truth may be helpful, but at this point, it feels like a man trying to tell them what to do. They don't know enough to trust you yet; and if they are struggling, they may have no practice confiding in a father figure.

We are not saying that other types of discipleship training are wrong—only that they are incomplete, especially for the demographic we are trying to reach.

It's not a problem with the truth but a problem with the skills needed to reach and serve a young man. For instance, Proverbs—the book of the Bible most focused on the rules for living well—is written from a loving father to his son (Proverbs 1:8). The refrain throughout the book—"my son"—is the expression of an authentic, deep relationship. The son trusts the father's love and can therefore hear his father's instruction.

The problem today is we too often want to give moral instruction without taking the time to build a positive, well-rooted relationship.

> *If you have never pursued a younger man to befriend and disciple him, you do not want to go in armed with just a few books, a Bible study, and good intentions.*

To develop an effective relationship with a younger man, to befriend and disciple him, never go in armed with just a few books, a Bible study, and good intentions.

We have seen older men get inspired to invest in the next generation. The passion and sincerity are there, but they soon find that their lack of training has not prepared them to 1) find a disciple, and 2) deal with the complexity of male relationships—especially intergenerational ones. They start by working through a book of the Bible or inviting a younger man to their church's event, but their efforts bear little lasting fruit.

This study will help you learn the *soft skills* necessary to become a spiritual father—not just *what* to communicate but also *how* and *when*.

Cultivating the soft skills of spiritual fathering will help you create a thriving relationship and offer biblical truth.

Modeling the Christian Life

When it comes to guiding younger men, we need to be willing to work and sacrifice. But we also need to do our best. Later in his letter to Timothy, Paul elaborates on what that looks like: "Do your best to present yourself to God as one approved, a worker *who has no need to be ashamed, rightly handling the word of truth*" (2 Timothy 2:15, emphasis added).

When Paul tells Timothy to do his best to have "no need to be ashamed," it should give us pause for self-reflection.

One of the things we have seen in our research is that younger men have a hard time finding older men whose lives are worth imitating. They see a lack of integrity.

Integrity

Man in the Mirror Founder Patrick Morley defines it like this: Integrity is a one-to-one correlation between my Bible, my beliefs, and my behavior. A lack of alignment can have devastating consequences for our character, witness, and lives—and certainly for a spiritual father-son relationship.

> *Integrity is a one-to-one correlation between my Bible, my beliefs, and my behavior.*
> **– Patrick Morley**

If you *can't* say with confidence that you have no need to be ashamed, spend some time reflecting on what's gotten out of place. For example, if you recognize a lack of integrity in your actions, then it's a safe bet that you will also see something going on in the core affections of your heart (your "belief system") causing that behavior. And if you don't like what you find in your belief system, you will probably find that something isn't lining up with the word of God.

Accuracy

The second thing Paul mentions is correctly handling the word of truth. To share scripture accurately with younger men, we need to be immersed in it ourselves.

But part of that immersion is modeling it. In Corinthians 11:1, Paul says, "Therefore imitate me as I imitate Christ."

As stated before, living a life worth imitating is not about obtaining perfection. But we need to be pursuing Christ and humbly confessing when we fall short. Only then will we be guides worth following.

Focus

Paul also writes: "Remind them of these things and charge them before God not to quarrel about words, which does no good, but only ruins the hearers" (2 Timothy 2:14).

When he says to "remind them of these things," Paul has just been writing about the gospel. Young men need us to correctly handle the word of truth and to keep reminding them of the gospel and how it shapes everything else.

Notice Paul also includes a warning here not to "quarrel about words." It is no accident that it's in the same sentence as reminding people about the gospel.

As we are focused on being spiritual fathers who exhibit both integrity and accuracy, it's vital that we do not get distracted by arguing over lesser things. This could include politics, cultural issues, or anything that keeps us from doing and being our best at fathering the heart of a son.

Our Journey

The rest of this study will be broken up into three main sections.

In chapters 3-5, we will explore the issues related to finding and growing your influence with a younger man. We will discuss the skills and steps required to meet, connect with, and cultivate a relationship with a spiritual son. This section is about getting started. We will explore communication habits of modern men. We will also look at some of the ways we want to be attentive to a younger man's needs.

In chapters 6-8, we look at what it takes to build a healthy foundation for your relationship as a spiritual father. We'll discuss the importance of setting boundaries and confidentiality expectations. We'll also give some keys to developing a strong relationship over time, including how to deal with emotions and hard conversations.

In chapters 9-12, we'll cover specific mentoring skills you'll need to practice, such as asking good questions and being an active listener. We'll discuss the importance of encouraging a spiritual son, and what steps to take when sin or poor judgement need to be confronted. The goal is not just to encourage being a voice of truth, but to help in understanding where to put the focus when spending time with your spiritual son.

The final section includes some short lessons on best practices and key points you'll want to remember as you prayerfully consider embarking on this journey. Thus, the purpose of this study is to help you learn more about how to impact the life of a young man by learning some soft-skills necessary to develop a strong father-son relationship.

We firmly believe that a spiritual father should be armed with both biblical truth and the soft skills of real parenting. When both elements work together, our sons will know real discipleship.

To be clear, this study is not a spiritual growth plan for you to use with a young man. Certainly, understanding and applying biblical truth is vital—and Man in the Mirror has extensive resources to help in these areas. In fact, we assume that you will incorporate some of those resources—and others—when the time is right to help your son grow.

Takeaways

- Discipleship is about more than head knowledge—for both the spiritual father and the spiritual son.

- The father-son relationship produces mutual growth.

- Never use the terms "spiritual father" and "spiritual son" when you're building a relationship with a younger man. This language is for internal use.

- The role of a spiritual father in the life of a son is similar to that of a mountain guide—going *with him* on the journey.

- The key to being an effective spiritual father is not skills or talent; it is love and trust.

- Humility is more powerful than perfection when it comes to guiding a younger man.

- Life experiences—both the successes and failures—are invaluable to a man who is further behind you on the journey.

- Part of being faithful to your calling as a spiritual father is doing your best to have integrity, accuracy, and focus.

Discussion

1) Have you ever had another Christian man give you rules and correction outside of relationship? How did it make you feel?

2) What skills do you think older men need most to spiritually father younger men?

3) What personal skills or experiences of yours might be helpful to a spiritual son?

4) What is a failure or struggle you experienced that might've been avoided if you'd had a spiritual father to guide you?

Prayer

Take a few minutes and share prayer requests around the group in the following areas: family, work, social, and personal.

Pray for the Lord to grow each of you in humility and grace, and to help each of you live a life of personal integrity, biblical accuracy, and missional focus on building the Kingdom of God.

Notes

ESTABLISHING
A RELATIONSHIP

CHAPTER 3

FINDING A SPIRITUAL SON

We begin with finding a son—the first and most crucial step in being a spiritual father.

As you read this, you may already have someone in mind. It may be a younger man from church that you have built up some rapport with, or it may be a man from outside your church, like the newlywed next door or the son of a friend who needs someone older to invest in him (that's not his dad). It might be a colleague or someone you talk with at the gym. It could even be someone in your own family, like a nephew, or even your own adult son.

If you don't already have someone in mind, the questions in this chapter are meant to guide you as you identify a potential spiritual son and some ideas on how to then initiate or grow the relationship.

Start with a List

Finding a spiritual son isn't like hunting hidden treasure. How many men do you know who are under 40? Simply put, every one of them is a potential spiritual son already in your orbit.

Start by taking an inventory of your walks of life and where you may interact with younger men already. Write down their names and begin to pray.

Once you've narrowed down the list (as needed), consider the following about each potential son—

Affinity: Do we share common interests?

It is certainly possible that two men with very different personalities and interests can build a connection. But having a few already apparent connections makes things easier when you are establishing a spiritual father-spiritual son relationship.

For example, if you love classic cars or basketball, then it makes sense that a younger man who shares your passion will be more likely to want to spend time with you. The same is true if you both work in the same career or industry. Shared experiences or interests help foster a sense of camaraderie and knits your lives together.

Faith: Is he a believer? Dechurched? New Christian?

It is important to understand your own heart and attitudes before you seek to help a younger man. A man who was raised in the church but has since walked away will raise different issues than someone who is new in his faith.

This is obvious but something to pause and reflect on before you offer to start a relationship. Not everyone is an evangelist or a scholar or an apologist. It is perfectly normal to feel drawn to someone in a specific stage of his faith journey. In fact, it is probably how God has wired you.

For instance, if you have experienced church hurt or a crisis of faith and come out the other side, you may be able to identify more with those who are dechurched and cynical. Or maybe you prefer to help a young believer grow and strengthen his faith. It is not common for someone to have the ability to serve men in both stages equally as effectively, so it's valid to weigh this at the start.

> *It is perfectly normal to feel drawn to someone in a specific stage of his faith journey. It may even be how God has wired you.*

No matter what kind of man you feel called to invest your life in, you can trust that God will give you the knowledge, strength, and wisdom you need to walk alongside him. And we will give you the resources and support you need to be effective with a man at any point on his journey.

Age: How much of a gap?

Age gap considerations fall into the same category as the faith of a spiritual son. You should weigh the ramifications of your differences before you begin.

For example, if you are in your late 60s and find yourself mentoring a young man who is 20, that is quite an age gap. There is no reason to avoid a large age gap, but it bears reflection before you start. It would be frustrating to begin this process with a much younger man only to find out you should have chosen a man in a later phase of life with whom you can more easily connect.

There is nothing wrong, in other words, with knowing where your talents and interests will flourish. Which brings us to—

Life Stage: Where is he in his family and career?

Every stage of life brings unique challenges. Consider these scenarios:

- A young single man is dealing with issues around dating, as well as a fear of being "left behind" by his friends, who are all getting married.
- A newlywed is having a hard time making ends meet, while also grappling with unmet expectations of what married life would be like.

- A man in his mid-30s is struggling to balance a new career, a marriage that has lost its pizzazz, three children under age six, and his shrinking circle of friends.

If you relate to certain life stages and circumstances over others and have your own hard-earned lessons and mistakes to share, seek out a younger man who can benefit from your wisdom and experience.

Struggles: Are you prepared to step into a crisis?

Some fathers are built for crisis and others are built for peacetime. If you are not yet capable of supporting a man who is going through a deep crisis in his life, then you should think about that before you begin.

> *Avoid trying to resolve situations that you are not qualified to handle.*

For example, if your heart and skills make you well suited to help a man facing divorce, infidelity, job loss, or a life-threatening illness, then you should be open to finding someone who is experiencing struggles of such magnitude. However, if you know this is beyond your skillset or capacity, take that into account.

But remember: *every* man eventually goes through a crisis, and that's when they need a spiritual father the most. A spiritual father can trust that the Holy Spirit will give him knowledge and wisdom as needed. (see 1 Corinthians 2:12-13).

Capability: Are his needs beyond the scope of the spiritual father-son relationship?

Connected to the previous question, avoid trying to resolve situations that you are not qualified to handle. This could be mental illness, severe addiction, or other complex situations that require professional help. You can certainly be a friend and father to someone in these situations, but you must know that a spiritual father is not a substitute for professional care.

NOTE: Throughout the rest of this study, you will see dialogue indented and italicized. These are meant to be examples of conversation, not scripts. As you read these interactions, think about how you might put these conversations in your own words.

> *This is a sample conversation. Please do not repeat it word for word. Make it your own!*

How to Be Proactive

Once you've made a choice to become a spiritual father and have a young man in mind, it is time to approach the potential spiritual son. The key here is to be proactive and plain in your words. Again, it is best at this point to avoid the terms "spiritual father" or "spiritual son."

Remember the phrase, "crawl-walk-run." Start with crawling. You're not going to ask someone you don't know that well to meet with you for a year or two. This would be a bit like telling a blind date you're hoping to marry her! Just tell him you'd like to hang out—

> *Hey, man. I'm wondering if you want to hang out sometime. I've got some free time and would love to grab a cup of coffee. No agenda other than getting to know you better. Can I text you and we'll get a time on the calendar?*

Depending on the potential son, an older man asking him to spend time together may be uncommon enough that it can feel awkward. In this case, it is often good to openly state you have no hidden agenda—and mean it. For the first time you hang out, your only goal is to connect and get to know each other.

Once a good foundation has been built, meaning your time together went well, you can ask if he'd like to add in some structure or intentionality—

> *Listen, I've got a few decades of experience. I am near the end of my career, I've raised kids, I've been through marriage challenges. I'm not an expert on life, but I have some vantage points I think you might find helpful. I'm wondering if you're interested in making this a regular thing.*

> *I'm not trying to "fix" you. I just know that I wish I'd had an older guy around for these years of my life. I'd love to hang out and do stuff together, but I'm also interested in being an ear for you no matter what the issue is. I know guys don't always share what's on their minds or going on in their hearts. I'm just an old guy here for you without judgment.*

Notice that in this example, the potential father is being clear but also soft in his approach. He is saying first and foremost that he wants some time together to get to know him better. He's not saying anything that suggests the young man is a screwup or has problems. And he is using his own experience—*I wish I'd had an older guy around*—as a foundation for his intentions.

Also note that he is still not suggesting that he wants to be like a spiritual father to him. Again, anything that feels like a formula to a young man—or like he is just a feather in your cap—is going to be met with suspicion at *best* and as an offense at worst.

Once you've been meeting for a while, you will increase the focus and level of intentionality during your time together—but not until a genuine relationship is formed.

In summary, avoid the mistakes of assuming 1) that you are a spiritual father before you've established trust and mutual affection, and 2) that you must delve into the depths of his life before he feels comfortable. You will bear incredible fruit if you take it slow and avoid violating the normal process of relationships.

Release Outcomes

The spiritual father-son relationship itself is not the primary end goal. Rather, the relationship is a *means* to the desired end—one of mutual growth, community, and transformation.

But you must be willing to release outcomes. In other words, let the Lord be in charge of the results. This is especially important if you are attempting to be a spiritual father for the first time. You must not let your eagerness to help another man become an idol for you. You are not the Lord, and remember, it is ultimately the Holy Spirit who brings fruit.

If you feel led to a potential spiritual son, you must be prepared for it to not work out. It's not uncommon to experience a false start in the earliest months of meeting. Nor does it mean the time you invested was in vain.

Paul stated it this way: "I planted, Apollos watered, but God gave the growth. So, neither he who plants nor he who waters is anything, but only God who gives the growth" (1 Corinthians 3:6-7).

Analysis Paralysis

A final note: As you consider these factors, don't get bogged down in evaluating every little thing about the person God might be calling you to approach. You'll analyze your way to inaction.

For one, you will never find a perfect match. But more importantly, you might miss the Holy Spirit's nudge toward a man who doesn't check all the boxes. When it comes down to it, the two most important factors in finding a spiritual son will be prayer and boldness.

If God has already put someone on your heart, approach him. And if not, make a list of younger men who might be interested in guidance from someone more experienced. Then use the questions in this chapter to narrow it to a few possibilities that you can pray about. Once you have clarity on *who*, invite him to get together for coffee or a meal, and watch what happens!

A Spiritual Father and Son Story –
Chapter Three: Frank Feels the Call

Sitting in church one Sunday, Frank heard an announcement that would change his life. They were looking for spiritual fathers to befriend and mentor younger men. Frank had been an empty nester for a few years and always felt like he could have been a better dad.

I'm sure they want guys that did a better job than I did, he thought. To his surprise, his wife nudged him and told him he should check it out.

Frank went to an orientation held at the church a couple of Saturdays later and felt compelled to give it a shot. He realized his mistakes with his own kids were lessons he had learned, and that there were many young guys out there who didn't have a dad involved in their life at all. He decided to give it a shot.

Frank thought through his various networks—work, church, neighbors, extended family—and narrowed it down to three names:

- Stephen, the young husband with two small kids who'd moved in down the street about a year ago. He was a graphic designer who worked from home. They'd had several casual conversations outside, and he'd even come in for coffee once.
- Sam, a guy from his church whom he'd gotten to know at a service project. He was a firefighter in his late 30s and seemed to be struggling in his marriage.
- Sean, his nephew, toward whom he'd always felt an affinity but never had more than casual conversations with at family events. His sister and Sean's dad had gone through a messy divorce when he was a kid. Frank remembered the time he'd had an extra ticket for a football game and invited Sean. They had a great time, but Frank never followed up.

Frank shared this list with a couple of guys who were also considering becoming spiritual fathers. After praying about it with them, they both encouraged him to start with his sister and ask about his nephew.

Frank called his sister, and she was thrilled. She carried around a lot of guilt that Sean had grown up mostly without a dad, and additional guilt that she'd not gotten the family involved with church. She told Frank that Sean had even mentioned his "cool Uncle Frank" a couple of times. "Cool for an old guy," she had kidded him.

At a family BBQ the next week, Frank pulled Sean aside and asked him if he would be up for lunch the next week. Sean said sure, and they set up a time to meet at a local Thai place.

Takeaways

- God has already put a spiritual son in your life. You just may not know who it is yet.

- A spiritual son can come from any area of your life: your workplace, church, neighborhood, hobbies, extended family, friends' sons, etc.

- Make a list of guys and think through them in terms of affinity, faith, age, life stage, struggles, and capacity.

- Don't get bogged down in trying to pick the "perfect" spiritual son. Pray and then go for it.

- Ask a guy to meet for coffee or a meal, not to be your spiritual son. Don't have a hidden agenda for those first times hanging out.

- Take the time to get to know each other and let the friendship progress naturally.

- Offer to be a listening ear. Share that you wish you'd had someone older to bounce things off when you were younger, and you'd like to be available for that.

Discussion

1) Do you have any reservations about approaching a younger man?

2) Which factor is the most important to you, e.g., "Age: How much of a gap?" Why?

3) Which Life Stage do you feel most drawn to, in terms of whom you have the most to offer?

4) Share your list of potential spiritual sons and ask for input.

Prayer

Take a few minutes and share prayer requests around the group in the following areas: family, work, social, and personal.

Pray over all the names on the lists you shared for potential spiritual sons. Pray that God would start making it evident to each of you what He wants you to do as you consider becoming a spiritual father.

Notes

CHAPTER 4

THE 1-2-3 METHOD OF COMMUNICATION

Not everyone counts the cost of discipleship. This is certainly true when it comes to the amount of time needed to connect and communicate with a spiritual son. Spiritual fathers can easily get tripped up by not realizing how much communication styles and practices have changed in the last decade or two. Assumptions are the problem here.

If we assume that younger men communicate as we do, then it can easily lead to miscommunication, confusion, or even frustration. But if younger men expect a different form or style of interaction, it would be good for us to explore this before engaging in discipleship.

Younger Men and Communication

Times have changed with technology. This is seen clearly when we explore how younger men communicate with each other.

For example, a younger man feels connected to the world around him. His routine is easy to follow. In the morning, he texts his mom a picture of the grandbabies. He is running a few minutes late, so he messages his boss to let him know. He arrives at work and starts his day, taking short breaks to look at social media and respond to a few posts. He sends a link to some buddies about the playoff game that night. Lunch is spent out or at his desk, all while scrolling through his phone, liking, commenting, or just browsing. The day ends and he leaves. He gets a message from his wife on the way home to stop and pick up a few things at the store. He finally arrives home for dinner. In his mind, he has connected with enough people to meet his needs for the day.

What is missing is authentic human interaction.

Men today rarely pick up the phone and talk, much less spend time face-to-face. This is ironic since men also spend an average of 3-5 hours a day on their phone or some other device. Watching videos, sending texts, checking social media, and so on.

Even when sitting with another person, they may not find the conversation stimulating enough and resort to looking at their phone. This is so prevalent that kids have coined this "phubbing"—snubbing someone by using your phone instead of talking.

Younger men do communicate with their peers, but it is frequently indirect and impersonal—at least by the standards of previous generations. For them, the best ways to connect are by text messages and social media interactions. They may consider another man their closest friend even if they rarely spend time with him in person. Friendships and closeness have been redefined.

> *Younger men do communicate with their peers, but it is frequently indirect and impersonal— at least by the standards of previous generations.*

This is supported by research on teens and young adults. Nearly half of them are online constantly. Almost 84% say they use their phone to "connect with others," but the same percentage of people also report using their phones to "pass the time."[11]

Even more striking is that a rather high percentage of young people (43%) use their phones to avoid people. If they find someone annoying or they just don't want to communicate, then it is perfectly acceptable to "ghost" them and ignore their messages.

They also use their phones to discuss important issues. A married man today is far more likely, for example, to argue with his wife by text message or to show his kids he loves them through social media posts. They announce both births and deaths by sharing links, and they send invitations to important events via email or text.

> *A young man's phone is central to his daily life and relationships.*

A young man's phone is central to his daily life *and* relationships.

Relationship Anorexia

It can be easy to scoff at younger styles of communication. *How can you be true friends with someone you never speak with in person or spend time with? Why can't you get through a meal without your phone on the table?*

The goal here is not to mock young men for their communication style or critique them for growing up in the modern era. Young men are a product of the times, and likely they don't even realize how starved they are for deep relationships—especially with older father figures.

For example, a recent study found that men between ages 18-29 view texting and calling as being of the same quality communication. The men studied spent an average of 287 minutes a day (almost six hours!) on their phone and sent roughly

---

[11]https://www.pewresearch.org/fact-tank/2019/08/23/most-u-s-teens-who-use-cellphones-do-it-to-pass-time-connect-with-others-learn-new-things/

190 text messages. They also viewed all forms of communication as identical. At no point did they find it necessary to spend large amounts of time physically near friends or loved ones.[12]

This is not a good thing. Not only has it created a spiritual depression in many younger men, but it's also exposed them to compulsive behaviors like playing video games excessively, binge watching television, consuming pornography, and other destructive habits that are done in isolation on personal devices.

This is the challenge we must step into: many young men are isolated, lacking relationship skills, and struggling to find real connection. Yet they may be locked behind a wall of technology.

Older men are not always up to speed or comfortable enough with technology to scale that wall. But you must be willing to engage a younger man on his level if you are to lead and care for him. We have to *go* to people, not expect them to *come to us*.

The Communication Burden of a Spiritual Father

Let's paint a picture to show the problem.

A spiritual father meets and agrees to spend time with a potential spiritual son. They set up the first meeting, and it goes fine. They chat a bit and share the basics—kids, background, career. They agree afterwards to meet again, setting a time to meet four weeks later.

In the meantime, the spiritual father doesn't contact him—no texts, calls, or other forms of messaging. Finally, as the date for their next meeting approaches, he sends an email reminder.

The second meeting is also fine. They share a bit more, but the son seems somewhat reserved and hesitant. They set a time for a third meeting—four weeks later. The spiritual father once again sends an email reminder a couple days before. Only this time, the son sends the father a quick reply about a scheduling conflict and apologizes.

It takes the father weeks to get the son to respond by email with a new time to meet. When they finally do, it still feels like they are strangers after three months. The relationship grows frustrating for the spiritual father, who starts to feel the spiritual son has no interest in building it. They agree to "do this again soon" but don't set up a firm time. And they never do.

The simple fact is, for the spiritual son, the spiritual father remains a stranger. He has not connected or communicated in a way the son is used to. The son

---

[12]https://www.kent.edu/kent/news/can-cell-phones-make-you-feel-less-connected-your-friends-and-family

rarely checks his email and never uses it to communicate with close friends or family. The father's attempts to use email therefore falls on deaf ears.

In the meantime, the younger man is sending dozens of text messages a day to those men who are in his network of close friends. And like it or not, he feels more connected to them than he does to the spiritual father he sees once in a blue moon.

If you experience tension or frustration over communication challenges, it's unhelpful and unproductive to spend time complaining. Yes, it can be startling at times to see how fast the rules of engagement have changed, but they *have* changed.

If you engage a spiritual son based on *your* preferences, you miss the chance to connect with him deeply. It may not come naturally, but, put simply, we as spiritual fathers need to use the most effective tools available to bridge the divide between older and younger men.

And here's the surprising truth—an upside—younger men's comfort level with "quick hits" of communication through text and social media will actually make it *easier* for you to keep in touch.

The 1-2-3 Method

Here is a simple plan for communication called the 1-2-3 Method, designed to give you success in the early stages of a spiritual son relationship.

Consider this plan to be the *minimum* effort required. It's a starting point. Effective communication with a spiritual son should include the following every month:

> *We are asking you to commit to this schedule— the 1-2-3 method— each month for an entire year.*

- At least 1 face-to-face time together
- At least 2 phone calls
- At least 3 text messages

Each interaction is like a deposit in the relationship account with your spiritual son. A proverbial "drip campaign" of connection. Take a moment and think about the power of this. You will be communicating with your spiritual son in some way *at least* six times per month.

The point of this method is to bridge the gap between how older men communicate and how younger men expect their close friends to communicate. You don't need to text hundreds of times a day or communicate on Snapchat (ask your son), but you do need to engage more like a younger man than perhaps you are used to.

This method helps to grow the relationship in-between face-to-face meetings, especially in the early months. Essentially the spiritual father needs to convey to his son that he is thinking of him and that he is looking forward to hanging out again. For younger men, four weeks feels like an eternity if there is zero contact.

A Note About Capacity

You may have the urge to dive into spiritual fathering with a vision of finding several young men to disciple at once. However, it's important to count the costs first. If you cannot maintain the 1-2-3 Method for *each* spiritual son every month with space for the relationship to grow, then you should reconsider.

If you have the time and capacity to take on more sons, then do so. But it is no problem to just focus on one relationship. The impact will be greater connecting deeply with one son than having shallow connections with three or four.

1 Face-to-Face Meeting

Spending time together regularly is most conducive to discipleship. It's the same model Jesus used—come and follow me, come and be with me, come and share meals with me. Come, let us be together.

Yet this flies in the face of many young men's preferences. Plenty of older men have reported that it can be excruciating to get younger men to commit to a day and time to hang out. This will improve with better communication between meetings.

Here are some additional tips to start out:

1) Make meeting times an agreed upon time that is always free for both of you.
2) Make the meeting place the same or similar each time.
3) Never leave without confirming the time and place for the next meeting.

The initial meeting should be focused on connecting and asking the basic questions you would ask anyone you meet for the first time. Do not try to counsel or go deep yet, especially if it is not happening naturally. Your posture for the first meeting is not that of a sage or a father, but a friend.

By the second or third meeting the conversation should start going deeper. A spiritual father's role should be first and foremost to ask questions and learn more about your spiritual son. You should also share about your own life, faith, and struggles.

At some point, doing an activity together can be helpful—shoulder-to-shoulder instead of face-to-face. Find an interest you both share like going to a sporting event, getting out on the water, playing golf, or building something.[13]

---

[13]For more ideas and pointers, see the Shoulder-to-Shoulder Activities section in Best Practices at the end of this Guidebook.

These shoulder-to-shoulder times can also be a good opportunity to teach a new skill. Younger men—especially if they didn't have a dad in the picture—sometimes struggle with doing basic repairs around the house, for example. If a spiritual father is skilled in some of these areas, it can be a significant bonding opportunity.

Never miss the fact that your role as a spiritual father will often mimic that of a real father. And with a generation of fatherless men, the more you can share your skills with a younger man, the better.

2 Phone Calls

Phone calls do not have to be long, but they do need to be consistent.

To help you be intentional, place two calls in your calendar each month and find a time the spiritual son is usually available to call and catch up. Most younger men tend to be free as they are finishing work or commuting, but before they are focused on family or personal time.

The call does not need to be about a specific issue—although it could be a call to follow up on something discussed at your last meeting. But it is enough to call simply to check in.

It is vital to get him on the phone rather than leaving a voicemail. Most young men do not leave voicemails, and his voice mailbox may very well be full because he never bothers to check it! Therefore, if you don't reach him, there's no need to leave a voicemail, because he will see who has called on the caller ID.

When you do get a young man on the phone, keep it light, personal, and brief. He may not be responsive if you call and barrage him with a lot of questions, or worse, if you just ask vague questions like, "How have you been?"

The best plan is to just share for a few minutes about your own life. "I have had a brutal week and not slept well but looking forward to going fishing this weekend." Or "My wife gave me a list of to-dos for around the house, and I thought I'd call you instead for a few minutes." You should feel free to monopolize the time of the conversation since, again, younger men are used to quick phone conversations.

This is a great way to model how a spiritual son can be free and open in conversation. The more you share about the regular parts of your life, the more he will share with you. It is an investment that does not pay quick dividends.

There can also be a specific question about something discussed at your last face-to-face meeting—a project at work, a kid's game coming up, or an event they were looking forward to. But don't plan on going deep during the call unless he initiates it.

3 Text Messages

Many young men often communicate solely through messaging apps. To avoid texting a spiritual son is to avoid connecting with him on his level, but texting shouldn't be used to avoid real communication. It should be a part of the communication, but not all of it.

The 1-2-3 Method means sending three texts (separate threads) a month between face-to-face meetings. This can be as simple as a few phrases or sentences, once or twice a week. Texts should be used as a simple touchpoint to convey that they are being thought of.

The three texts shouldn't be reminders of an upcoming meeting. While a text reminder can always be sent, this is not the same as the regular text messages in the 1-2-3 Method for the purpose of connecting.

Text messages should be lighthearted and casual. Focus on mutual interests, such as, "Did you see that game last night?" Send links, funny memes or gifs, or something else informal. Tell him briefly what's going on in your life ("Spending the weekend with the grandkids. Haven't seen them in a long time so I'm excited.") or share a photo. Be real and relatable. And steer clear of politics or culture wars; younger men are exhausted by those topics.

It is essential that confidential or sensitive information is not sent via text. For example, if a spiritual son confesses that he is having difficulty in his marriage, do not send *anything* about this via text. You can imagine what would happen if someone read this out of context. Or worse, if his wife was unaware that he had opened up about this with you, only to see the conversation via text. There should never be a reason for a spiritual son to doubt the confidentiality of the relationship.

The importance of text messaging is that it allows you to connect briefly on a social level. It is not important that you get a response or start a long conversation. The spiritual son may not respond, or it may take a few days for him to respond. This is normal for younger men. Consistency matters more than his responsiveness.

> *Your consistency matters more than his responsioveness.*

A Spiritual Father and Son Story – Chapter Four: Communication Rhythms

Frank and Sean decided to meet up for the first time at a local coffee shop. They found out they share a connection over vintage cars and a love for college football. They talked briefly about their wives, kids, and careers. Before they parted ways, they agreed to meet again—same time and place—in four weeks.

After that day, Frank sent a few text messages to Sean but was disappointed when Sean either didn't respond or just sent a thumbs up. Sean also didn't answer the phone the first couple of times Frank called.

The next time they met up, Frank swallowed his pride and asked him, "Do you mind that I texted you a few times this month?" Sean surprised Frank by saying, "No, it's great! I really appreciate you reaching out. I saw that you called a couple times, too. Sorry I didn't answer. I don't really talk on the phone that much. But if you call me, maybe try later in the evening. I'm more likely to pick up."

In the weeks after their second meeting, Frank continued to send a text each week, and they actually had one string of messages back and forth discussing an upcoming family get-together. The week before their third meeting, Sean answered the phone when Frank called one night around 8:00. They had a nice, short conversation and confirmed their meeting the following week.

By the end of the third month, Sean was answering both Frank's texts and calls almost every time—and even initiating a few of the texts himself. They had established an easy rhythm of interaction that felt friendly and comfortable.

Takeaways

- Communication between face-to-face meetings is vital to sustain and grow a relationship.

- A good standard to use is the 1-2-3 Method: A monthly minimum of 1 face-to-face meeting, 2 short phone conversations, and 3 text messages.

- Face-to-face meetings are more sustainable if they are scheduled at approximately the same place and time each month, so they can become regular.

- Take your time establishing trust and vulnerability. It may take several meetings for the conversation to go beneath the surface.

- Think about doing some "shoulder-to-shoulder" activities as well, centered around a common interest, such as playing a round of golf, or offering to help him do a home repair he mentions.

- Don't leave voicemails. Just call back later.

- Text weekly at least. Share an update or follow up on a previous conversation.

- Be careful what you write in a text message (e.g., talking about a marriage struggle is unwise via text since his wife is likely to see his phone).

Discussion

1) Is there anyone in your life beyond your family or coworkers that you communicate with intentionally at least weekly?

2) What forms of communication are you prone to struggle with or find difficult?

3) Would it be difficult for you to commit to weekly communication with a spiritual son?

4) Talk about where you plan on meeting. What are the pros and cons of meeting in a coffee shop versus your home or a workplace setting? What other ideas do you have for meeting?

Prayer

Take a few minutes and share prayer requests around the group in the following areas: family, work, social, and personal.

Pray over your lists of potential spiritual sons. Share any changes to your list before you pray.

Notes

VULNERABILITY + SAFETY + TIME

This chapter includes critical information about the overall *approach* to spiritual fatherhood. Too many older men think that advice or teaching alone is all that's needed to help a young man. They prefer to be a sage who dispenses wisdom—spiritual laws and nuggets they've picked up along the way.

There is a time and place for spiritual laws and life lessons, of course, but young men can already find plenty of it in sermons and podcasts. What they are lacking is a restorative and healthy relationship with a spiritual father figure—an older man with whom they can discuss all aspects of life, from the mundane to the profound. They need someone who can encourage their healthy habits while also supporting them in areas of brokenness that need correction and restoration.

This approach of the overall discipleship relationship takes a longer view of the amount of time and trust needed to bring about real change and growth. Building this kind of relationship will require at least three ingredients: Vulnerability + Safety + Time.[14]

Vulnerability

Vulnerability connects us to other people. It is what separates a deep, authentic friendship from a polite, pleasant acquaintance.

To be vulnerable is to be your honest, real self, rather than the pretend self we may present to strangers at parties. It is the difference between a real conversation about life and small talk. Between putting up a front and letting someone see the real you.

As men, most of us were not taught how to connect deeply with others—least of all with other men. At some point, we were taught not to cry, not to show weakness, and to mask our emotions behind a guise of strength. We learned that to avoid rejection from friends, we should hold back our true struggles or fears to keep it comfortable.

All of these inhibit vulnerability. Instead, what we want to develop with a spiritual son is the ability to connect deeply. This includes sticking our necks out and running the risk of being rejected.

---

[14]For a similar way of talking about pastoral ministry in the church, read Ray Ortlund's blog here: https://www.thegospelcoalition.org/blogs/ray-ortlund/gospel-safety-time/

Take for example a man who has lost his job. Wearing the typical mask, he might spin the story: "It just didn't work out. It's not what I wanted to do anyway; I'm fine."

But as a spiritual father, we want to encourage and demonstrate the freedom to say the truth: "It hurt that I lost this, and I question my talent to move forward in this career."

It also requires vulnerability to show love and affirmation to another man—a rare occurrence for most. Many men find it awkward to give another man a compliment, or even say they admire or respect each other. But we must, as spiritual father figures, show ourselves to be both capable and comfortable with this, nurturing the relationship by expressing love and respect freely, *with words*, on a consistent basis.

> *Remember, vulnerability is not a tactic for spiritual fathers. Rather, vulnerability is a way of life that we all need to embrace.*

Remember, vulnerability is not a *tactic* for spiritual fathers. Rather, vulnerability is a way of life that we all need to embrace.

Grace and Vulnerability

Beyond our basic human need for vulnerability is the truth of the gospel. When God purchased us, He didn't just buy the "pretty" parts. He paid for ALL of it: the past, the sin, the shameful stories, the messes, and the failures. The cross strips off our masks and the defenses that we use to hide our sin. If we are to be good men, we are to be men before the cross. And if we are to be good spiritual fathers, we must begin with a strong sense that we are imperfect.

Our raw imperfection—that real sense of sin—is what provides the frame of reference to lead younger men.

Don't think you must have led a perfect life, made only good decisions, and never caused anyone pain to be a good spiritual father. On the contrary, to pretend you have arrived at your current station in life without acknowledging the thorny path that brought you there is to deny God's grace in your life. And in doing so, you withhold the lessons that grace has taught you. The most effective lessons you can share come not from your successes, but from your failures. All of us are prone to similar temptations and mistakes, and where you have fallen, you may keep a younger man from going down the same path. But to do so, you must be prepared to be transparent.

Transparency is like cooking with hot peppers; a little goes a long way, and you must be careful how you use it. The extent to which a spiritual father shares his shortcomings should be appropriate for the level of the relationship. Sharing too much too early can be harmful to the relationship. Also, he should use caution in sharing the details of his failures. Discretion and discernment are key here.

Instead of skipping over the ugly parts of your story, carefully use them as signposts of God's mighty work in your life to illuminate the path for your spiritual son.

> *Our raw imperfection—that real sense of sin—is what provides the frame of reference to lead younger men.*

A Conscious Choice to Be Real

All it takes to be vulnerable is a conscious choice to speak freely—to drop the mask and be the real you. By doing so, you can help lead a younger man into this same freedom.

Here are some ways to do this:

Model the Behavior you Want to See

Paul tells his spiritual children to imitate him as he imitates Christ (see 1 Corinthians 11:1). But this is what children do naturally, too. Watch any young boy around his father and see how he mimics him.

Vulnerability starts with the spiritual father, and it starts with being mindful of the need to model this behavior. This modeling is both verbal and by example.

Verbally, a spiritual father makes it clear after a period of time that he doesn't want a relationship that is merely pleasant and chatty. When appropriate, ask the extra question, and be ready to answer one from him. As your relationship grows, discuss with him that you want to be real, or vulnerable, or honest—whatever word you find suits you best.

As an example, be vulnerable when you're with him. Don't say you want to be honest and real, then be vague or coy yourself. You need to lead here and lead strongly. Even if your spiritual son is slow to catch up or hesitant to be vulnerable, it is on you as the father figure to continue demonstrating it. Think "long term, low pressure."[15]

Keep inviting him to be honest, and don't react negatively if he is reluctant. It may be months before a spiritual son lowers his guard—especially if he hasn't had a father figure in his life. The goal is vulnerability over time, and sometimes that time takes longer than we hope. Stay the course.

---

[15] This is a key idea discussed in the Sustain Momentum Through Relationship chapter of the book *No Man Left Behind*. The chapter is focused on long-term discipleship and the importance of giving guys time to open up.

Admit Your Flaws Openly

There is a generational gap between what older men and younger men tend to focus on in our conversations. Older men typically like to talk strengths and successes. They describe the highpoints, the places where God has gifted them with talent to accomplish goals in life. It's not as if older men *deny* their flaws or failures, but generally, they talk about the blemishes less often.

> *In a culture that celebrates victimhood, we need men who acknowledge their shortcomings and avoid blaiming others.*

Younger men as a group tend to go the other way; talking about their flaws is the natural posture of someone who is real and unpretentious. Because of this, they may be less interested in how you succeeded than they are in how you struggled.

For example, if you are talking with your son about your marriage, you should be just as clear about the areas in which you struggle as you are about your strengths. It is incredibly inviting to your son when you admit these things in humility, like, "I have trouble dealing with my wife's intense emotions sometimes." Or "When I get lazy around the house, my wife gets frustrated asking me for help, and I need to improve in this area."

This tells your son that you are a real person and that the issues he has in his marriage are normal. As you model vulnerability and admit your flaws, he is learning that a real man is honest and real and takes responsibility, rather than being guarded and blaming someone else.

In a culture that celebrates victimhood, we need men who acknowledge their shortcomings and avoid blaming others as much as possible.

Ask Forgiveness Frequently

Another area we can model appropriate behavior for a man is in our readiness to ask for forgiveness. If you arrive late to a meeting, are slow to respond to a text, or say something that gets taken the wrong way, apologize—for offenses both big and small.

Men today are brash and headstrong, and we have a pattern of holding back when we should be free to ask forgiveness. Let your spiritual son know why you want to be freely asking for forgiveness.

In addition, tell your son about the times you ask forgiveness from your wife, kids, or others. For example, if you had a fight with your wife last week and put your foot in your mouth, share the story of how you apologized. It's possible that he has never seen a tenderhearted husband or had apologizing well modeled to him.

Share Your Stories of Hurt

Relating with a spiritual son about your weaknesses is one thing, but you should also find space to discuss times you have been let down, hurt, or mistreated. This, too, is a normal part of the human experience.

Maybe a boss mistreated you, a pastor or spiritual leader let you down, a friend betrayed your trust, or your kids hurt your feelings. Men love to stuff these stories down and ignore the pain of being hurt—or we reach for anger or denial.

But we need to show our spiritual sons how we dealt with these hurts in healthy ways—or how we didn't and learned from it. Even in cases where you should have responded better, or where anger got the best of you, share the story with a sense of remorse.

A spiritual son is likely to have similar stressors and needs in his life, and the more you share, the more likely he is to share his hurts with you. This does not mean that you trash your wife, nor does it mean you give yourself license to unburden every grief you have with everyone. But it does mean you are honest about the challenges that relationships come with.

It takes a strong man to be vulnerable. If we are going to be effective as spiritual fathers, this is the kind of strength we want to model.

Safety

Men growing up with father wounds, or without fathers at all, have experienced a lack of safety. This isn't referring to a lack of physical safety, though plenty of men grew up without physical protection or with physical abuse.

Rather, too many younger men are unaccustomed to the warmth of a father's comfort. They have rarely had an older guy for a confidant. They likely, too, have never had someone to share their sin or brokenness with—or even their bad habits.

Young men need to feel safe with their fathers. But if they have not known this safety before, it will take time to cultivate. Most men are hiding serious issues in their lives—darkness that needs to be brought into the light. The only way this can happen is if he feels safe.

He can frequently be reminded that he should share these things—or even be asked pointed questions about where he may be struggling with pornography, drinking, or other behaviors. But safety can't be forced.

A sense of safety stems from a combination of love, commitment, and confidentiality.

Confidentiality

Once he does feel safe enough to be vulnerable, you want him to fully trust you with whatever he shares. He must know for certain that anything he shares will stay between the two of you.

Today, the world feels increasingly public. Social media and other online tools allow people to have access to our lives in a way unheard of for most of history. Beyond that, we tend to cultivate a persona for people on social media—sharing the good parts of life and avoiding the painful or sinful parts. We are good at hiding in plain sight.

This is especially true for men under 40, who may do this instinctively, having spent such a large portion of their lives online. It might appear from the outside that their life and career are going well and that their marriage is on solid footing, but the reality may be far different.

These issues make it crucial to establish a sense of confidentiality with a spiritual son. It's not the case that every young man has deeply rooted issues, but you must be ready for that reality. And if he can't talk to you, who will he share it with?

Clearly state that you are committed to confidentiality—and occasionally reaffirm that commitment.

> *I want you to know that I will maintain confidentiality with anything you share. This means I won't tell my wife or pastor or anyone else what you share with me without your permission. I have no judgment for what you may be struggling with in terms of sin and brokenness. You cannot shock me or disappoint me.*
>
> *I will be honest with you about my stuff, too. I have screwed up and sinned a lot in my life. But I've experienced grace and restoration. And if I can trust you with my past, I hope you can trust me with your present.*

This relationship is about more than simply having fun and sharing life. With time, it will hopefully involve sharing deeper parts of yourself—and that requires trust and confidentiality.

Some of the deepest pain that occurs in the context of one-on-one discipleship—or with pastors and spiritual leaders in general—is caused by the breaking of confidence. So be committed to your spiritual son's privacy.

Exceptions (Legal Disclaimer)

Abuse

There are two instances where you are required as a spiritual father to break confidentiality: if there is illegal activity or if there is a threat to someone's safety.

Any confession of abuse must be taken to the authorities. If, for example, your son confesses to any abuse at all involving his partner or a child—you must get help immediately. Do not do this alone. In fact, you should already know the person you will call if such a situation presents itself. Ideally, you will have both a pastor and a professional counselor to lean on for advice.

To be clear, there must be no "sweeping it under the rug" when it comes to abuse of any kind.

It is your legal responsibility to seek help in the case of abuse. A professional will be able to guide you on the next steps for confronting the situation and possibly getting the proper authorities involved.

Suicide or Self-Harm

Self-harm is a delicate issue, but it's just as important to know your legal responsibility. Any threat of self-harm—suicide or even the ideation of ending one's life—must be taken seriously.

In most cases, these fantasies of ending it all come from a place of pain. He may not be legitimately planning on taking his life. But any comment about suicide must be met with love and support, including professional help.

The same preparation is useful here, too. You should know who you would call in this situation beforehand.

It is also important as a father to broach the topic with your son proactively if he is in a dark season. For example, if your son is going through a divorce, the loss of his career, the death of a loved one, or another tragic situation—it is important as his spiritual father that you ask him directly if he is struggling privately with thoughts of taking his life.

> *I know you are going through a lot right now. It's normal to have dark thoughts in these situations. But I need to know: are you having thoughts of harming yourself or ending your life? It's nothing to be embarrassed or ashamed of if you are, but I want to get us professional help if that starts to happen. So please just be honest if this is happening.*

Many lives have been saved and restored by someone brave enough to ask another person if he is struggling.

Time

Few things ruin discipleship more than the tyranny of the urgent. We want deep relationships quickly, for our advice to be heeded immediately, and for sanctification to be smooth.

The gospel doesn't work that way.

You need to be prepared for the relationship to evolve and progress over months or even years. The process of change in a man's heart and life happens at his pace, not yours. When you are feeling impatient and frustrated, pray for the Holy Spirit to give you patience and grace. Don't put *your* expectations for change onto your spiritual son.

You can set a high bar in your own mind for where you would like him to be. You can have hope for a quicker pace of growth. But you should never communicate impatience or allow cynicism to take root in your heart.

And if you think about the trajectory of your own life, you'll likely see it's been marked by slow growth,

> *God is pleased to work slowly and deliberately in our lives.*

setbacks, and at times sudden breakthroughs. God is pleased to work on His own timetable, and that is often slower and more deliberate than we might want it to be.

Observation Over Time

Israel was often told to set up monuments and markers to remember the work of God in their history. And Christians have, ever since, found ways to remember the works of God.

We are committed to the idea that God is pleased to work slowly and deliberately in our lives—like a mustard seed. Nourishment and growth can feel unrewarding if we do not give ourselves guideposts along the way.

Here are three practices that will be helpful for you as a spiritual father:

Journal the Journey
Keep a prayer log and reflection journal about the time spent with your spiritual son. Keep it at least weekly, even if you only write a few sentences. After one-on-one time, you should take time to journal more extensively. Write down impressions, conversation topics, sore spots in your son's life, ways you can pray for him, and areas where you see growth.[16]

It is important that the journal be honest about what you are seeing—the good, the bad, and the ugly. You should also journal how this relationship is affecting you personally. How is God using this to help you grow? What lessons are you learning? How has it helped you see things clearly in your own life?

Keep it confidential. Although this can be a helpful tool to use on your own or in your small group with other spiritual fathers, you should not show it to your spiritual son.

Reflect Quarterly
If you journal regularly—even if you are not always consistent—you need to review the journal from time to time to get a sense of progress.

Set a reminder in your calendar to review your journal quarterly. Read through your reflections, think about any patterns you see, and remember what issues arise.

---

[16]For more on journaling, see the Best Practices section in the back of this Guidebook.

Share Your Discoveries

While your journal itself should remain confidential, it is helpful to share good insights you see with your spiritual son. As you review your journal, jot down notes separately on lessons learned or progress made that you might want to share.

For example, if you get to the end of a year and you notice a pattern of growth in your spiritual son as a husband and father, this should be brought to his attention. Let him know that you notice growth in that area and are happy for him.

Or if he continues to struggle in one specific area, you can note with him how long of a journey it's been.

Vulnerability + Safety + Time is a simple formula but a difficult path to follow. You will likely violate these principles if you've never thought about them or experienced them yourself. But they are also guideposts to help you get back on track. And as you more intuitively implement them in your practice as a spiritual father, they will bear much fruit!

A Spiritual Father and Son Story –
Chapter Five: Getting Vulnerable

It had been six months and things were going well. But Frank sensed a kind of plateau in their relationship. He and Sean got along well, and they had great discussions, but Frank felt like it wasn't going as deep as it should by now.

A couple days before their next meeting, Frank had a string of minor difficulties. He missed a major deadline at work, and while he wasn't worried about losing his job, he did feel like he had let a lot of people down and that his reputation had been damaged. Feeling that frustration, he had spoken sharply to his wife and started a fight over something that had been bothering him. In the process, he had really hurt her feelings. And then the trifecta: driving to work frustrated the next morning, he had run a red light and got a ticket.

Sitting down with Sean, he was relieved to have someone to talk to about all of this. They had become decent friends. Frank shared about his work failure and how that had affected him with his wife. And then how the ticket had been the icing on the cake.

Sean looked at him and said, "Wow! I thought I was the only person things like that happened to. So, if you don't mind me asking, how'd you resolve things with your wife? I could use some help with that, too."

They talked longer that day than they ever had, and Sean opened up about some things going on that he hadn't yet shared with anyone. Frank told him he understood firsthand the risk of letting things fester, so he encouraged Sean to give him a call or set up a time they could talk through it when he found himself in that state.

Frank noticed a new openness with Sean in the weeks that followed. It was almost like a spigot on a hose that got another half turn. Frank realized that he and Sean had a safe relationship that had taken time—*months*—to build. And as their friendship deepened, so did their ability to be open and vulnerable with each other.

Takeaways

- Three keys to being an effective spiritual father are vulnerability, safety, and time.

- Vulnerability is being real, honest, and open in appropriate ways.

- One of the biggest obstacles to vulnerability is our cultural tendency to avoid expressing emotion or weakness.

- The key to vulnerability for a spiritual father is to remember who you are in Christ.

- Modeling vulnerability to a spiritual son will include admitting your own flaws, asking forgiveness, and sharing your own stories of hurt.

- Safety stems from a combination of confidentiality, love, and commitment.

- Maintaining your son's confidentiality is paramount. The only exceptions would be in cases of abuse or self-harm (actual or threatened).

- Discipleship and change take time—a long time.

- Establishing guideposts through journaling, quarterly reviews, and discussion will help you as a spiritual father.

Discussion

1) Do you find it a challenge to listen to others without judgment?

2) How does your identity in Christ help you be vulnerable with your spiritual son?

3) What are your expectations for how a relationship might progress with a spiritual son?

4) If you have acquired one, take some time to look at the known spiritual fathers journal together. This will give you a framework for journaling, quarterly reviews, and sharing your discoveries with your spiritual sons.

Prayer

Take a few minutes and share prayer requests around the group in the following areas: family, work, social, and personal.

Continue to pray over your spiritual sons lists—that God would guide you to the right decision about engaging as a spiritual father.

Notes

FOUNDATIONS

CHAPTER 6

BOUNDARIES

It's important for the spiritual father-son relationship to be built in a healthy way. To do this, clear boundaries must be set. Any relationship that doesn't is likely to suffer—or even end in disaster.

Good boundaries build good trust. All our relationships—whether with our spouse, children, friends, colleagues, or neighbors—include boundaries—both spoken and unspoken.

As a result, you probably have a working knowledge of the value and importance of boundaries already. But here's a look at boundaries from the angle of spiritual fathering.

The Basics

A boundary is any rule or space we create to maintain our own identity and wellbeing. They protect a person from harm, control, or manipulation.

A boundary serves as a line between two people, delineating how much power you allow someone to have over you, and how much power you have over that person.

As a child of God, you are His workmanship and created in His image. No one has been granted the right to manipulate you or make unhealthy demands on you, or to require of you more than God has required of you.

Even more importantly, having good boundaries will remind you of your role in the life of a spiritual son. You are not God, and you have not been given the job to behave as if you are. Setting and keeping healthy boundaries will help you maintain your rightful place as a spiritual father who is dependent on his Heavenly Father.

> *Setting and keeping healthy boundaries will help you maintain your rightful place as a spiritual father who is dependent on his Heavenly Father.*

Boundaries can be flexible. You may have a few that are set in stone, but it's natural for them to need fine tuning over time, depending on the circumstances.

The purpose of having boundaries is not to isolate yourself or create a sense of division between you and your son. Rather, it's to maintain your peace while also serving a younger man as a spiritual father.

Boundaries with Your Family and Your Time

There are two foundational rules of boundaries for spiritual fathers.

First, do not do anything that makes you or your family uncomfortable against your will.

If you have a family, your primary job as a husband and father is to care for yourself and your family well. This might look like reminding your spiritual son that you are not available to him around the clock. Late night calls or unannounced drop ins are allowable *if* you allow them, and some spiritual fathers are fine with a more relaxed arrangement. What you want to be mindful of, however, is a son who pressures you from a place of neediness or anxiety.

You also need to have clear permission from your wife and children if you are planning on bringing him into your home. Hopefully, as the relationship grows, your son will feel free to come around your family and be invited into your life. But if your wife or kids aren't on board, you need to engage in further discussions with them first. Otherwise, the situation would only lead to awkward interactions. Or worse, your son might feel unwelcome, leading to a strain on your relationship.

Second, do not do anything that confuses your son about your proper role in his life.

The previous chapter outlined the 1-2-3 Method of communication, but you should also be clear about what communication is *not* allowed. This is a personal question, but one you must answer. Are there times when you want to be unplugged and unavailable? Will it be detrimental to your family life if calls come in at certain times, such as during dinner? Communication boundaries will vary based on the spiritual father's preferences but consider them carefully and make them clear.

It also bears repeating that in cases where your spiritual son has certain needs around mental health or impulsive behaviors, it is not your responsibility to try to deal with emotional or psychological issues on your own. And you should always safeguard the wellbeing of your family first.

Types of Boundaries

Boundaries can be physical, emotional, relational, or spiritual.

Physical Boundaries

Physical boundaries are literally about the space around our bodies. Some of these boundaries are obvious; for instance, no matter how angry anyone becomes, there can never be any violence or threat of violence.

It's rarely a problem that men need extensive physical boundaries when it comes to affection. If anything, men need to *increase* the amount of physical affection they show each other—especially between fathers and sons. You don't have to greet each other with a holy kiss (Romans 16:16), but hugs and pats on the back are certainly appropriate.

You should, however, think about the role of physical boundaries in two key areas: with families and in terms of personal space or property.

Over time, your spiritual son will hopefully have some level of interaction with your family. Like any other good friend, you would want him to feel comfortable coming to your home for a meal or including him in a family activity when it makes sense and is appropriate.

When it comes to personal property boundaries, consider what financial arrangements work well for you. For example, it is important to determine ahead of time if you are able and willing to pay for your son when you meet for a meal or do something fun together. A misunderstanding in this area has the potential to be uncomfortable or embarrassing for both of you.

Emotional Boundaries

Emotional boundaries are tougher to define and keep. When most people today discuss boundaries, they mean emotional boundaries.

Emotional boundaries might seem complicated, but they are actually pretty simple:

- Don't allow anyone to manipulate you using your/their emotions.
- Don't manipulate anyone else using your/their emotions.
- Don't take responsibility for someone else's emotions.

For example, the sense of discomfort we feel when someone tries to "guilt trip" us is often our internal sense of a need for a boundary. A good emotional boundary recognizes, *you may want me to do something, but you do not have the power to make me feel guilty if I don't let you.*

Refusing to take responsibility for someone else's emotions keeps a spiritual father from falling prey to the idea that they are the only thing keeping their son together. This results in an unhealthy distortion of the relationship.

Spiritual Boundaries

Spiritual boundaries involve our faith and our role as a spiritual father.

One way we keep our spiritual boundaries is by not sacrificing our biblical views for the sake of harmony. But we need a clear distinction between essentials and non-essentials here. On the non-essentials we can be at perfect peace with our sons if they have different opinions or are uncertain about what they believe on that issue. Arguments over the mode of baptism or the best form of worship music, for example, are unlikely to be fruitful (see 2 Timothy 2:23-24). But on the essentials of faith, we maintain our boundaries by being clear about what our convictions are.

Remember: Your spiritual son does not need a theological lecture. In fact, for most young men, this is the *last* thing they need.

What he needs is love and mentoring based on the convictions of your faith. And if the opportunity presents itself, then yes, you should be ready to discuss biblical or theological subjects and how your beliefs impact your life.

> *To force any beliefs onto our sons is spiritual abuse. Our role is to encourage, support, and admonish.*

You may disagree even on major, fundamental theological issues. If you do, it's not the end of the world. Your spiritual son may not even be a believer, but as long as you are clear on your convictions, you should be able to maintain the relationship.

But most important is maintaining a correct view of your spiritual role in his life. This boundary is critical. As spiritual fathers, we are not given authority to dictate, demand, or force our opinions onto our sons. To force any beliefs onto our sons is spiritual abuse. Our role is to encourage, support, and admonish.

Remember the guide analogy from Chapter Two. You are with him on a journey. Maintain your convictions and allow him to have his as well. It is not your job to change his heart. That is the job of the Holy Spirit.

Relational Boundaries

Relational boundaries are any relationships we will not share with our son or any relationships our son will not share with us.

As discussed already, we need permission from our families to invite our sons into our personal lives if that's desired, and we also need to maintain boundaries with our spiritual son's family and friends.

Discovering Your Boundaries

Issues for spiritual fathers arise when they go in blind, having never thought about their boundaries before. In this case, if a spiritual son begins to behave in a way that the spiritual father is uncomfortable with, it may feel as if it is too late to consider and establish boundaries.

Knowing your boundaries ahead of time empowers you to express yourself clearly and set the pace from the start. Please take time to consider the following:

- Are there certain times I do not wish to be available in the evening?
- Are there certain times I do not wish to be available during the day?
- Is there a limit to how much money I am willing to pay for my son when we hang out? If so, what is that limit?
- Am I willing to have my son in my home?

- Am I willing to have my son around my wife and kids?
- Are there any health issues that might slow me down?

If you have the desire and ability, allowing a spiritual son into your space is hugely beneficial. For example, a young man who is newly married without kids can learn so much by being around an older couple who have raised kids, who have been through hell and back in their marriage, and who know what it takes to thrive later in life.

We strongly encourage spiritual fathers to consider this relationship as more than just having coffee or a meal together occasionally. Bringing him into your home and around your family or friends whenever possible and appropriate can be life changing for a young man

Note that this isn't required. Your own family dynamics and the other demands on your time are important, personal factors. If you can't say yes to something, then don't say yes.

Expressing Boundaries

The best way to frame your boundaries is to put them in an "I" statement, rather than a "you" statement. Be clear and matter of fact.

For example, say, "I am unable to talk after 8 pm. But I promise I will do my best to get back to you within 24 hours."

Do *not* say, "You call me too much at night. You should find a better time to call me."

Most of the time, people are perfectly willing to abide by boundaries when explained clearly. The real hurt occurs when a person's boundaries are not communicated, and others are left to guess at the person's motives.

Early in the relationship, a spiritual son needs to know what you are and are not willing to do. These should be basic rules about how you will interact and respond to his needs and requests.

Symptoms of Poor Boundaries

The symptoms of poor boundaries are subtle at first, but they tend to get serious quickly. Here are a few:

- A sense of unease at the urgency of a spiritual son's needs.
- It weighs on you that you can't always be there for him at a critical moment.
- You have moments of anger or frustration that he is becoming "too much" for you to handle.
- You're finding the relationship more and more exhausting.
- You're less than honest with him about your feelings.
- You begin to feel resentment rather than affection for him.

You may be susceptible to having unclear boundaries if you often have trouble saying no to things. Many men are "people pleasers" without realizing it. If you worry about not meeting others' expectations at the expense of your own needs or those of your family, or if you often find yourself overcommitting because you don't want to let anyone down, this is something you'll have to work to overcome.

> *Most issues that develop from poor boundaries could have been avoided by clear communication. And that communication starts with the father.*

Spiritual fathers with poor boundaries are often trying hard—sometimes too hard—to keep the relationship going. They may like the feeling of being needed, and before long, a desire to help gets distorted into a burden to rescue.

The weakness here is a lack of clear and healthy communication. The father does not speak up about what he is and is not able to do for his son. And so, without knowing where the boundary is, the son steps over it during moments of pain or neediness, asking for more than the father can give.

As the boundaries continue to break down, the son may sense the father pulling away and struggle to keep the relationship going amid fears that it is slipping away.

Like in this scenario, most issues that develop from poor boundaries could have been avoided by clear communication. And that communication starts with the spiritual father.

Be clear from the start and throughout your relationship about what you are capable of in terms of your time and other resources. Plenty of young men will be content with occasional breaks during the week or knowing there are certain times you aren't free to talk.

But you cannot, you must not, go hot and cold on him, showing up in some moments and then ghosting him the next. It will eventually damage the relationship beyond repair.

Correcting Mistakes in Boundaries

So, you find yourself in a relationship with poor boundaries. Do you cut and run? How do you fix things?

The answer is to work toward making a course correction gently but firmly—and with as much love as you can muster. Take the following approach if you need to reestablish boundaries—[17]

---

[17] The following example may feel contrived—no one actually talks like this—but we are intentionally writing it to make sure the components of correcting a mistake are fully expresses. Of course, you will put this in your own words should the need arise.

Confess Your Shortcomings

It is important that you model humility and respect, and nothing signals this more than taking ownership of the situation. If you struggle with pride—and we all do—it can be easy to avoid this step and rush to establish your boundaries. But it is important to let a spiritual son know that you take responsibility for the pattern of miscommunication.

Spell out the situation as you have perceived it.

> *Hey, you texted me a few times in the late evening and seemed frustrated when I didn't answer right away. I know in the past I've always replied right away, even late at night, but I need to be more present with my wife in the evenings. I realize that I may have come across that I didn't care or that I ignored you. That was not my intention.*

Truly Apologize

Offer your apology sincerely and truly. Let him know his feelings matter and that if you disappointed him, you are sorry.

Even if you don't feel you did anything seriously wrong, it's more important to show him you value his emotions. Remember that you are modeling a father's behavior, and your son may have deep father wounds. This is an opportunity to show him the standard of biblical accountability.

> *Remember that you are modeling a father's behavior, and your son may have deep father wounds.*

> *I wanted to apologize for any disappointment I may have caused you. I know you may say this is no big deal, but you're a big deal to me. I want you to know that I'm sorry and I want to help make things better.*

Confirm Your Love and Commitment

Following your apology, use this opportunity to reconnect and reaffirm the relationship.

> *I really value our time together and want to keep investing this time together. It brings me a lot of joy.*

Establish or Reiterate Your Boundaries

After the emotional and restorative work, you should establish or reiterate your boundaries. Please note that this is the last thing you do, not the first.

A boundary without love is just a cold rule. But if you've shown him you care about him, you may now clearly state a boundary.

Okay, so my boundaries are simple. I will almost never answer the phone or respond after 7 pm, since that is dinner and family time, and sometimes I'm just worn out. I'm a morning person, so I may write back to you the next day. If I can't get back to you fast, I promise I will as soon as I can.

One Final Note

Keep in mind that the spiritual father-son relationship is a reciprocal one. This means that your son may have boundaries of his own. If he communicates a boundary to you, commit to respecting it.

A Spiritual Father and Son Story – Chapter Six: Establishing Boundaries

Frank and Sean meet each month at a sandwich shop that is convenient for both of them. The first time, Frank picked up the tab since he had invited Sean out. The second time, Sean got there a few minutes late, and Frank paid again without thinking. Without intending to, Frank had started a pattern.

They had done a few activities as well—an evening at one of those multi-level driving ranges, a basketball game, and even a movie. Frank paid for it all.

Frank was thinking about an upcoming activity for them to do, but to his surprise, he felt reluctant. After thinking through his feelings, he realized he was a little resentful because Sean had only offered to pay one time and hadn't offered since. Frank knew he had to talk to Sean before it festered and undermined his enthusiasm for their growing friendship.

At their next lunch, Frank got his courage up and laid it out. "Sean, I've realized something that I need to tell you about and apologize for. I have been picking up all the expenses for us whenever we hang out, and I'm fighting a feeling of feeling taken advantage of." Sean looked surprised and something else… Confused? Guilty?

Frank continued, "You haven't done anything wrong. I've just taken on the responsibility of paying for everything without ever asking you about it. I'm happy to pay for most things, but if you're able, it would be good for you to maybe plan some of our activities into your budget."

Sean thought for a second and said, "Of course! I'm sorry. I realize I have just fallen into a rut of letting you pay for things. I have even felt guilty about it at times but haven't known what to say. I don't want you to think I feel entitled or that I'm taking advantage of you. I'd like to pull my own weight the best I can. Actually, that brings up something I've been thinking about. Can you help me make a budget? I've never really been very good with money."

"I'd love to!" said Frank. And their relationship took another step forward.

Takeaways

- Healthy relationships require clear boundaries.

- Good boundaries build good trust.

- Boundaries protect you, your family, and the spiritual son.

- Warning signs that your boundaries are unclear may include frustration with the relationship, feeling burnt out or resentful, or an inability to be honest about your concerns.

- Setting healthy boundaries will require forethought and clear communication.

- Boundaries can be physical, emotional, relational, or spiritual.

- Emotional boundaries are the most common area of difficulty. This includes when you feel that you are being made to feel guilty over something that you have no control over, or for setting a firm limit and sticking to it.

- Setting spiritual boundaries means that we don't have to agree on every theological issue, but you are going to stand by your convictions.

- The best way to express boundaries is with "I" statements.

- When you realize that you have poor boundaries, it needs to be addressed quickly and humbly.

- Respect any boundaries that your spiritual son sets for the relationship, too.

Discussion

1) Do you struggle with maintaining healthy boundaries or asserting your needs?

2) How do you typically respond when someone crosses a boundary? Do you tend to be a people pleaser? Do you grow cold and distant? Elaborate.

3) What are some specific guidelines you would set for each of the four types of boundaries (physical, emotional, relational, spiritual)?

4) Looking at your list of potential spiritual sons, has God added or removed anyone? Discuss any changes.

Prayer

Take a few minutes and share prayer requests around the group in the following areas: family, work, social, and personal.

Continue to pray for God to show you who the right man is on your list.

Notes

CHAPTER 7

ATTACHMENT STYLES

To be successful as a spiritual father, it is important to establish a strong bond—a relationship like Paul's and Timothy's—based on mutual trust and affection. This is sometimes easier said than done. If you are struggling to connect with the young man you are meeting with, to get past the shallow small talk or have a consistent relationship, you may want to consider what his "attachment style" is.

When it comes to discipleship, you will find it helpful to have some understanding of the role of attachment styles. An attachment style is a set of instincts we each have in our relationships—and each style is built on our past relational experiences, particularly in our formative years.

Were we raised in a loving home with a strong connection to our parents? Did we have rich and rewarding relationships during our childhood? Were we the outcast, or were we popular with our peers? The answers to these kinds of questions factor into our attachment style.

Simply put, are we able to have a secure connection to the people we love, or do we struggle to create deep bonds? Just as our attachment style impacts our family relationships, so too does it impact our discipleship relationships.

Please note that this chapter is by no means exhaustive on the subject matter. The aim is simply to introduce you to four primary attachment styles as they relate to discipleship and the spiritual father/son relationship.

The Basics: Trust and Esteem

One of the most helpful ways to think about attachment styles is to look at two factors in a man's life: trust (how he views others) and esteem (how he views himself).

A person with high trust and high self-esteem tends to be likable and confident. He is secure in his identity and boundaries, and thus, able to form secure relationships—or "attachments." But if either of these two factors is a struggle, forming relationships will be more challenging for him—in fairly predictable ways.

As a result, there are four attachment styles. Two are high trust, which means they are more likely to seek out **engagement** (though one does so in a healthier way).

1. Secure: high trust and high esteem
2. Anxious: high trust and low esteem

The other two styles are low trust, and they tend to be **avoidant** when it comes to deep relationships.

3. Dismissive: high esteem and low trust
4. Fearful: low esteem and low trust

The matrix below shows these four styles and how they relate, as well as the approximate percentage[18] of adults who have each one:

	Avoidant	Engagement	
High	Dismissive (20%)	Secure (50%)	Self-Sufficient
Esteem			
Low	Fearful (5%)	Anxious (25%)	Needy
	Low	High	

Trust

1) Secure Attachment Style

This is the ideal way to live in relationships. A person with a secure attachment style knows what love feels like, they can internalize it, and they receive love without any major hurdles.

They feel secure in relationships and trust their loved ones. As a child, they knew the love of at least one parent—a love that was not withheld or doubted even during hard times. They connected with peers well and formed at least one lasting friendship. They never had reason to doubt if they were loveable. *Even when they made mistakes, they always had a secure sense that they were not being rejected.*

This connection type is also ideal in a discipleship relationship. A man with a secure attachment style is easier to form a bond with. He shows up willingly to meetings. He lets his guard down easily and is not afraid to get real. He can be alone

---

[18]A broad review of the research gives a range on the percentage of adults in each group. We are using the consensus from various sources, as well as our own experiences, to come up with these percentages.

for a season without feeling lost or anxious. He has a strong sense of self-worth and can regulate his emotions.

Because a secure person feels safe with you, he is more likely to trust you in your role as a spiritual father. He internalizes his own value and receives your affirmation with ease. If you admonish him in an area of his life, he listens and trusts your words. His self-esteem is such that he takes correction well, desiring to grow as a person.

> *A person with a secure attachment knows what love feels like, they can internalize it, and they receive love without any major hurdles.*

A broad review of the research shows that approximately 50% of people have secure attachment styles. If your spiritual son is one of them, it does not mean that everything will be smooth sailing or perfect. But it does mean that the foundation for a relationship is easily established—and once established, the relationship is secure.

2) Anxious Attachment Style

A person who has low self-esteem but a high desire for engagement is likely to have an anxious attachment style. This person wants a relationship but is fearful of abandonment. This can translate into an unhealthy reliance or neediness.

Lacking any sense of their own worth or value, they can become preoccupied with you as the person who can help. As a spiritual father to a son with an anxious attachment style, you can become a life preserver—or worse, you become like a messiah to them. You are the one who will give them comfort. You are the one who will save them. Without you, they don't feel they can make it.

> *As a spiritual father to a son with an anxious attachment style, you risk becoming a life preserver, or worse, becoming like Jesus to him.*

Children who experience physical or emotional abuse are often likely to feel this sense of anxiety about relationships. They were perhaps emotionally starved or isolated. Growing up, they never knew what made someone mistreat or reject them, but now they assume everyone will leave them eventually.

This can manifest in adulthood in several ways. Their relationships with women may tend to end with rejection. They may never have had any close friends to help them learn to communicate. They may have trouble at work because they never stop people pleasing or feeling hurt and victimized.

The anxious disciple is prone to violating your boundaries. They might call or text at all hours, and their messages make it sound like the sky is falling.

For the anxious disciple, there is an endless hunger for validation—so much so that it can feel to the spiritual father as if your praise and support are never enough. You praise them one day, and the next day they again seem down and in need of validation.

They also tend to be passive; yet they never quite seem to be listening. They want to please you since they feel it is the only way to keep the relationship, but at the same time, they don't respond well to criticism, becoming defensive or angry. In such situations, they will push you away before you can do them any harm.

The anxious person may also be inclined to follow various gurus, including writers, preachers, podcasters—*anyone* who can help them navigate the anxiety in their head. However, they never seem to achieve lasting peace. Starved for real connection, they instead opt for a stable of wisemen with whom they have no relationship.

In many cases, these discipleship relationships are difficult to maintain. The anxious disciple often can't stop looking for validation, even after you've given it multiple times. He also may suddenly find another person to be the focus of his needs if he feels the need for more validation.

Experts believe approximately 25% of adults have an anxious attachment style. If your son is one of them, setting healthy boundaries, as discussed in the previous chapter, will be crucial if you hope to have a meaningful and relatively healthy relationship.

Maintaining the boundaries won't be easy. Compromise them and you could feel quickly overwhelmed and even manipulated. At the same time, maintain them very strictly and you might be accused of being mean or rigid.

Try to do your best to be consistent, firm, and loving, and reach out to other men for support and feedback when needed.

Commonalities of the Avoidant Attachment Styles

The man with one of the avoidant attachment styles— "dismissive" or "fearful"— doesn't trust you. But don't feel bad; he has a hard time trusting anyone!

As you might imagine, if you don't trust others, you will avoid putting yourself in situations where others can hurt you. This creates a unique challenge for a spiritual father.

The causes of this type of attachment style are complex, but often it involves an upbringing that was marked by neglect or abuse. Children who come from adoption, divorce, or who struggled with a parent's chronic illness are frequently found in these categories. Their emotions were either rejected or unnurtured. Crying was scolded, ignored, or there was no parent to cry to. In the absence of strong connections, they grew up believing that the hunger of loneliness was normal.

These characteristics tend to be more pronounced in men, who have long been under the pressure of a culture demanding they be stoic and emotionless.

If your spiritual son displays one of the two avoidant attachment styles, he may have a strong stubborn streak. At the point when, normally, a relationship would grow deeper and more transparent, there is a tendency to hit a wall. Problems do get shared and discussed, but he may lack the basic emotional vocabulary to express himself. Because the avoidant son has never known these skills or was told repeatedly to keep his issues and needs private, he will drift away if allowed to.

> *In the absence of strong connections, they grew up believing that the hunger of loneliness was normal.*

3) Dismissive Attachment Style

When a man with low trust has high esteem, his style may be dismissive. The dismissive attachment style, prevalent in about 20% of adults, can be summed up by the phrase, "I'm good."

These men may appear self-sufficient and aloof—or even too cool to need relationship. You can see an example of this in the 1997 film *Good Will Hunting*, where the main character, Will, has suffered abuse and uses his humor and intellect to keep everyone at arm's length. But the pattern is so common in younger men that it almost needs no explanation!

The dismissive avoidant son may be incredibly funny or smart. But, like Will, they use these skills as a *mask* since it is easier than acknowledging their emotions. Ask a serious question and you get a joke or philosophy.

> *The dismissive attachment style can be summed up by the phrase, "I'm good."*

For spiritual fathers, this attachment style can be frustrating because the spiritual son may do whatever he can to keep the relationship casual. He will no-show meetings or come unprepared. And once there, he will hide behind the façade of being successful, since the vulnerability of sharing the struggles of life is too daunting.

4) Fearful Attachment Style

Living in fear in a relationship is a killer. And some avoidant attachment styles show fear more than anything else. The root causes tend to be the same as *dismissive* avoiding. The difference for this small group is that fear drives the son to attach to the father in unhealthy ways.

The fearful man will hide his faults from you—afraid that you will be angry and reject him. Or he may not even be aware of the faults. His lack of self-esteem may result in a shocking lack of insight. His defense mechanisms are well-honed and difficult to penetrate. You have a long road ahead.

These young men may have more sensitive dispositions, and many of them never had a father. The spiritual father's approval becomes what matters most, and they are desperate to hold tight to the relationship to make things right in their lives.

Someone with fearful attachment style may appear shy, quiet, or uncertain around you since he is afraid of letting you down or saying the wrong thing. Or he may verbalize his fears, concluding that you are the only thing keeping him afloat.

The foundation of this relationship is not a healthy father-son connection but rather fear. Thankfully, this is the rarest of the attachment styles—about 5% of adults.

> *Someone with fearful attachment style may appear shy, quiet, or uncertain around you since he is afraid of letting you down or saying the wrong thing.*

Fathering a Secure Son

While it may seem easy to form a strong bond with someone who is secure in their attachment, there are still some guidelines that will help you foster a close relationship.

The first thing to remember is that, while someone may form secure attachments, there is nothing that says how *fast* the connection will be made. In fact, any attempt to rush the relationship may backfire. He knows what a close friendship feels like and how it naturally progresses.

> *Secure sons will not tolerate insincerity, slacking off, standing them up for meetings, or not following through.*

Secure sons will not tolerate insincerity, slacking off, standing them up for meetings, or not following through. This is because they likely already have strong relationships—with family or close friends—and will spend at least some time verifying that you are worth their time.

The important part of any relationship is building trust and empathy toward each other, and this reciprocity is especially true with a secure son. Share your story, your life, and your faith. Relate to his struggles with your own struggles, past or present. Give a secure son the time to grow roots with you and build the secure attachment they are capable of.

Fathering an Anxious Son

Even early on, an anxious son will show a need for constant reassurance. If you begin to suspect this attachment style, do not worry as much about establishing hard boundaries in the early stages. He's not a time bomb waiting to go off. Focus instead on letting him know you're reliable.

The initial goal for your relationship should be creating a sense of security. However, this can be developed while you are also showing him that your role isn't to rescue him.

Find the courage to be like Paul, who can lead with conviction but still feels the freedom to call himself "chief among sinners" (see 1 Timothy 1:15). You are going show up for your son, but you will not be the anchor of his spiritual life. It is perfectly good to raise this point with him if he is anxious.

> *Do not worry as much about establishing hard boundaries in the early stages. He's not a time bomb waiting to go off. Focus instead on letting him know you're reliable.*

You want him to believe you're not going to abandon him. But you also want him to know that you're not perfect. You're just a regular guy who's seen a lot in life.

The most important part of your relationship with an anxious son is to remember that you are not his savior or rescuer. The more he thinks you are, the longer it will take to develop a healthy relationship.

This can be hard for new spiritual fathers. It feels good to feel needed, so much so that as the relationship progresses, we can grow blind to our need for boundaries. But if you do not eventually place limits to preserve your time and energy for your own needs and family, you may get sucked into a black hole of need.

How would you eventually address this ongoing anxiety in a spiritual son? Slowly and carefully. The challenge here is that people with anxious attachment style tend to be hypersensitive, since the basis of your relationship, they feel, is a direct reflection of their own worth. Anxious sons are likely to put up a barrier when they feel criticized and will act like they don't care. (In fact, this style is sometimes called "Anxious-Ambivalent" for that reason.)

When he's doing this, it's helpful if you're able to continue to be normal and casual around him. Someone who is anxious tends to avoid real connection, ironically, by only talking about dramatic or negative things. Don't let him hide in the drama. In these moments, steer the conversation back to everyday life.

Above all, if you are trying to connect with someone who is severely anxious, you must be prepared for things to be difficult at times. It is normal, for example, for your boundaries to confuse or anger them. But be patient, gentle and firm. Your stability and love for them will draw them back.

And if they *do* choose to walk away, it is not your fault. There is only so much you can do to maintain a relationship that is fraught with uneasy feelings. But be sure you're lifting it up in prayer regularly and doing what you can to build a healthy relationship.

Fathering a Dismissive Son

If you suspect your spiritual son has a dismissive attachment style, prepare to do a lot of heavy lifting in the early stages of building the relationship. He may appear emotionally flat, distant, or uninterested—or he may mask his style with shallow warmth. It will feel like pulling teeth to get him to text or call you back and expect some plans to be cancelled at the last minute.

> *If you suspect your spiritual son has dismissive attachment style, prepare to do a lot of heavy lifting in the early stages of building the relationship.*

It should always be in your mind: *This person has not been loved well, and I want to help.*

During your first couple of times hanging out, avoid initiating heavy conversation. You'll probably not get a straight answer out of him anyway! If you ask how he's doing, you're going to hear "fine." The walls are up, and no amount of effort is going to bring them down—yet.

Dismissive sons also do very well in situations where there is a shared experience. If they can be shoulder to shoulder with you, having fun, they will start to warm up. Find out his interests and plan something enjoyable that has the potential to create stories that bond you together.

Another thing that helps is involving him in your life. Your spiritual son may not have had an example of the role of a healthy man in his family. Bring him to your home, ask him to help you do some work around the house, and make him a part at some level of your family life. (This is good practice no matter what his attachment style might be.)

It is crucial in a relationship with an avoidant son that you keep your word and show up. Naturally suspicious, he is hardwired to quit and will start out in the relationship with one foot out the door. He will also assume your initial interest in him is insincere. So, if you have schedule issues or problems with communication—if it takes you days to respond to a text or you no-show him—then an avoidant son will live in the quiet pain that you, too, are rejecting him.

The solution to all these issues will be time, consistency, and modeling vulnerability.

Demonstrate what emotional honesty looks like by sharing your own life and struggles a little at a time. For example, you might share that you have had a rough week and feel a little conflicted by something that happened at work. Or that you had an argument with your wife that the two of you are working through.

For a spiritual son who may have been emotionally starved for much of his life, it will be refreshing for him to converse with someone who is a little raw. Eventually he will feel safe enough to share his struggles as well.

Fathering a Fearful Son

If you suspect you have a fearful son, you will need a mixture of affirmation and boundaries. Maybe your phone regularly blows up with calls and texts when he needs something. Or perhaps you praise him one day, and the next he behaves as if you think negatively of him. It's as if his heart is dry soil that never absorbs the truth that he belongs.

If this is happening, this spiritual son needs to know that he is genuinely cared for. Be generous with your praise and encouragement. But there also needs to be a mutual respect for each other's time and availability. Remind him that you are just one man and that you want to build a healthy relationship.

If the spiritual son is especially fearful, you should remind him often that you are with him for the long haul—that even if you are unavailable at times, he will not abandon him

That said, you mustn't feed the situation by allowing yourself to be at his disposal nonstop. The goal is for your spiritual son to feel confident in your relationship, not give in to the false belief that he can't function without your constant attention. Just as with an anxious son, setting good boundaries is vital to creating a healthy relationship with a fearful son.

Father Wounds and Other Factors

A lot of helpful material has been written about father wounds.[19] Attachment styles are often the consequences of these wounds.

But there are many factors that influence attachment styles. A boy's relationship to his mother (both individually and in the context of his parent's relationship—or lack of it), his schooling, economic conditions, and childhood loss are just some of the ways that attachment styles are formed.

Depending on a spiritual son's background, talking about these formative experiences could become a regular topic throughout the relationship. You don't need to press, but make sure you pay attention when he brings up a memory from his past. He wouldn't mention it if it isn't important, even if he doesn't realize it.

---

[19]Author and pastor Robert Lewis teaches about this in his series, *The Quest for Authentic Manhood*, available from LifeWay. Lewis also wrote a bestseller that can help dads avoid wounding their children, *Raising a Modern Day Knight*. Though written for fathers of boys, there are many carryover concepts in the book.

Know Yourself

Certain kinds of questions can help gauge where a man is in his ability to feel secure with a spiritual father.

> *Having greater awareness of how past experiences still influence you will make you more effective as a spiritual father.*

It may also be helpful for you to explore some of these patterns in your own life that might impact your relationship. We all have wounds and experiences that can affect our attachment style and relationships skills. Knowing how your past has impacted you will help you walk alongside a younger man as he may be dealing with the impact of his past.

Below you will find a series of questions that probe our attachment patterns. Answer the questions honestly, and then reflect on those answers you either strongly agreed or strongly disagreed with.

As you do this exercise, pay attention to what is going on in your heart and mind as you consider each question. Does it bring up any feelings? Do you find yourself not wanting to complete it? Does it make you think of past experiences you haven't thought about for a long time?

Feel free to grab a journal and record any thoughts or feelings this exercise brings up. Then discuss it with other the other men in your small group.

Having greater awareness of how past experiences still influence you will make you more effective as a spiritual father.

Origins

1. I had at least one parent with whom I always felt secure and loved.

   Strongly Agree   **Somewhat Agree**   **Somewhat Disagree**   **Strongly Disagree**

2. I don't remember feeling alone as a child very often.

   Strongly Agree   **Somewhat Agree**   **Somewhat Disagree**   **Strongly Disagree**

3. I had at least one strong friendship growing up.

   Strongly Agree   **Somewhat Agree**   **Somewhat Disagree**   **Strongly Disagree**

4. As a child, I had at least one person I could turn to when I needed advice.

   Strongly Agree   **Somewhat Agree**   **Somewhat Disagree**   **Strongly Disagree**

5. I felt like my childhood dreams and development were celebrated.

   Strongly Agree   **Somewhat Agree**   **Somewhat Disagree**   **Strongly Disagree**

6. Growing up, I had an older man that helped me develop into who I am today.

   Strongly Agree   Somewhat Agree   Somewhat Disagree   Strongly Disagree

7. I was encouraged as a child to communicate my wants and needs.

   Strongly Agree   Somewhat Agree   Somewhat Disagree   Strongly Disagree

8. Discipline and punishment for me as a child were always done with love.

   Strongly Agree   Somewhat Agree   Somewhat Disagree   Strongly Disagree

If most of your answers were on the left "Agree" end, you had what is generally considered to be a healthy childhood. You were secure in your relationships with your parents and friends, your accomplishments were noticed and praised, and your mistakes were corrected lovingly. You are not typically suspicious of others (high trust), and you were given a healthy view of yourself (esteem).

If most of your answers were on the right "Disagree" end, you probably had a more difficult childhood and may have felt lonely much of the time. This is not abnormal, but without further reflection—perhaps through conversations with your wife, pastor, or a counselor—you may have issues with believing the best about yourself or others.

Relationships

9. I have rarely had positive relationships in my life where I felt safe, known, and secure.

   Strongly Agree   Somewhat Agree   Somewhat Disagree   Strongly Disagree

10. My wife (or girlfriend, ex, etc.) complains that I am closed off or unwilling to get too close.

    Strongly Agree   Somewhat Agree   Somewhat Disagree   Strongly Disagree

11. I have acquaintances but few deep friendships.

    Strongly Agree   Somewhat Agree   Somewhat Disagree   Strongly Disagree

12. I would do anything to keep my loved ones happy, and I tend to always put them first.

    Strongly Agree   Somewhat Agree   Somewhat Disagree   Strongly Disagree

13. I can't stand it when someone I care about is upset with me or disappointed.

    Strongly Agree   Somewhat Agree   Somewhat Disagree   Strongly Disagree

14. I often argue with explosive words in a loud voice; I just get so mad when someone is against me.

    Strongly Agree   Somewhat Agree   Somewhat Disagree   Strongly Disagree

15. I sometimes wonder if I care about people more than they care about me.

    Strongly Agree   Somewhat Agree   Somewhat Disagree   Strongly Disagree

16. I prefer to rely on myself and rarely reach out to others for help.

    Strongly Agree   Somewhat Agree   Somewhat Disagree   Strongly Disagree

This time, the scale is flipped. If most of your answers were on the right "Disagree" end, you tend to have healthy, deep relationships with others. You are likely in the "secure" quadrant of the attachment styles chart. Your security in relationships will help you in your role as a spiritual father.

If most of your answers were on the left "Agree" end, you probably struggle with having satisfying relationships. Don't be ashamed; many men find themselves here. Realizing this can help you work on your relationships. Talk this over with your small group, as well as your spouse, pastor, or a counselor. And pray! Allow the Holy Spirit to bring you the reassurance of your loving heavenly Father who created you.

You can use this tool to reflect on your habits and internal motivations in a relationship. Think about your tendency to avoid or engage in relationships (how you feel about others), and your own self-sufficiency or desire for validation (how you feel about yourself).

Please note there is no right answer for how you attach to another person. But if you find that you lean in one direction, then it's worth reflecting on, especially as you seek to be mindful of a spiritual son's needs.

If you both find the subject relevant to your relationship and want to go deeper, you can explore these styles together using quizzes that are available from multiple online sources—but not until you've met a few times and established some rapport.

Grace and Our Attachment Styles

A lot of this chapter has been about how brokenness influences our relationships. It can be discouraging to experience the challenges that come with certain attachment styles.

But instead, let it inspire compassion and love. Men who have trouble connecting to others securely need trusting and loving fathers in order to learn new ways to be vulnerable in their relationships.

And we too, as spiritual fathers, have our own challenges when it comes to this. Few of us are experts. As we grow, our spiritual sons will grow, too. And as the barriers to deeper discipleship relationships fall away, we can more fully share our lives together and experience vibrant lives in Christ.

There is nothing final or fatalistic about how we attach to another person. We are not doomed to be locked in a cycle of broken relationships—especially when we are in Christ.

> *There is nothing final or fatalistic about how we attach to another person. We are not doomed to be locked in a cycle of broken relationships— especially when we are in Christ.*

The hope is that we will see healing and restoration wherever needed in our lives— and that this chapter will prepare you to better understand and serve a spiritual son. In God's grace, we will be "stirring up one another to love and good works" (see Hebrews 10:24) and growing in our trust of God and each other.[20]

A Spiritual Father and Son Story – Chapter Seven: Frank Says the Wrong Thing

Meeting with his small group, Frank shared that Sean had been increasingly needy lately. Frank had felt gratified in the first few months of his mentoring relationship with Sean. They had connected over shared interests and extended family, and Sean had opened up about the heartache of growing up without a father.

But for the last month, Sean seemed to be growing more and more reliant on Frank for reassurance and validation, calling him about even the most mundane decisions he needed to make and engaging Frank in long conversations. Frank had tried to set some limits with him when needed: "I have about 10 minutes, Sean. What's up?" But each time, Sean just charged through the available time and kept on talking.

One day at the office, in a moment of stress and tension brought on by work, Frank had gotten very short on the phone. "Sean, you keep calling me about problems you're perfectly capable of handling on your own. And when I say I only have a few minutes, I mean I only have a few minutes! You're wearing me out!"

After a moment of silence, Sean had mumbled an apology and said he had to go. Frank felt terrible. He knew Sean honestly valued his advice and had, for the first time, a father figure to talk things through with. And Frank had squashed him.

---

[20]For another clear example of difficult attachment styles, spiritual fathering through them, and God's healing, search the Man in the Mirror website for the article **In His Own Words: A Man Transformed**.

His small group listened and commiserated with him over the situation. But then one of the guys said, "Hey. This is a great opportunity for you to show Sean what it's like to own a mistake and make amends. Just go to him and apologize. Tell him you feel bad about speaking sharply and that you really appreciate how much respect he has for your advice and counsel. Then discuss how you can offer that input in a way that's helpful to him and manageable for you."

They brainstormed how that conversation might go, including some ideas like texting questions instead of calling, to give Frank some time to think through his answers, and a regularly scheduled phone call each week to talk through things.

Frank also realized that he actually *liked* guiding Sean through decisions. It was just that he was in a stressful season at work that was leaving him more strapped for time, sensitive, and short-tempered.

He called Sean and asked him to meet for coffee the next week—earlier in the month than they usually met. Frank apologized to Sean for snapping at him and asked him for forgiveness. Sean seemed stunned. He stammered through a response and started to apologize back. Frank stopped him:

> *You have already apologized to me, and I accept your apology. I want you to know that I really do want to help you make wise decisions. And I appreciate that you want my opinion!*
>
> *So how about this? Let's text each other once a day. You let me know what you're thinking about. I'll text you back if I have ideas or input. But I need you to be patient. If I've got stuff going on at work or home when you text me, it might take me a few hours to get back to you. But I* will *get back to you.*
>
> *Then, let's just plan on having a phone call every week on Wednesday mornings. I'll call you around 7:30 on my way to work and that will give us a half hour to talk. If there's anything else, we can connect over the weekend on a call or make plans to hang out.*

Sean looked at Frank and said, "You sure? I don't want to bother you." Frank assured him it was a good solution and realized that it would take some time on this new schedule for Sean to believe that Frank really wanted to talk to him—just at times that worked for them both.

Takeaways

- An attachment style is a set of instincts we each have in our relationships—and each style is built on our past relational experiences, particularly in our formative years.

- A person with high trust and high self-esteem is able to form healthy, secure relationships—or "attachments."

- But if trust or self-esteem (or both) is a struggle, forming relationships will be more challenging, leading to dismissiveness, anxiety, or fear.

- Understanding the four primary attachment styles in this chapter will help prepare you for both the opportunities and challenges you might face early on and throughout the relationship building process.

- Understanding the four styles can also help you recognize your own patterns and be more effective as a spiritual father.

- No matter what attachment style you or your son have, God can redeem and restore our broken places so that we can experience the security of His love, as well as meaningful discipleship relationships.

Discussion

1) Do you personally identify with any of the four attachment styles in this chapter?

2) Review your answers to the self-assessment questions in the Know Yourself section. Did this bring up any issues for you? Did you learn anything about your own experiences that you hadn't considered before? How would this help you in a relationship with a spiritual son? How about in your other close relationships—i.e., with your wife, children, extended family, or friends?

3) Is there an attachment style you think would be exceptionally hard for you to engage with?

4) How helpful would it be for you to realize the attachment style of a spiritual son? Why?

Prayer

Take a few minutes and share prayer requests around the group in the following areas: family, work, social, and personal.

Pray for each other about any issues this chapter may have revealed—for the Holy Spirit to bring healing where needed.

Continue to pray for your list of potential spiritual sons and that God would direct you the right decision about becoming a spiritual father.

Notes

EMOTIONS

As we all know, there are plenty of jokes about men being unable or unwilling to express their emotions. Since Adam, men have tended to withdraw. There's a reason we all want our very own "man cave."[21]

But there is nothing inherent in us as men that prevents us from expressing our emotions. Men aren't born emotionally closed off; these are learned behaviors. Young boys are openly emotional, free with their tears and laughter, capable of going from sadness to joy with relative ease.

The good news is, if our stoicism is a learned behavior, we can unlearn it. As spiritual fathers, we must work toward properly dealing with emotions in our own lives so that we can help spiritual sons properly deal with emotions in their lives.

The Importance of Feelings

Make no mistake. Men feel emotions.

Go to any football game. Men shout with joy at a victory in the championship, they yell in anger at the referees for a missed or incorrect call, and they occasionally shed a tear when their team loses an important game. In those moments, no one could say that men repress their emotions.

Closer to home, men feel joy and happiness without a problem. If their child performs well in a competition or their relationship with their wife is fulfilling, men are happy, and they easily show it.

But there are certain kinds of emotions that men are less comfortable with. The difficulty comes with harder emotions that require vulnerability. Men have cultivated a macho sense that certain emotions are a sign of weakness.

Research on this has revealed the toll this lack of emotional life is having on men. There is a "relational gap" that grows in men as they progress into adulthood. Almost as a rite of passage, their childhood emotions grow cold in favor of a model of manhood that prizes toughness.[22]

This progression into a more "macho" version of manhood can lead to a mild form of depression. Our wives are usually the first to notice this pattern in us.

---

[21]There is a term in psychology for this phenomenon: normative male alexithymia. Literally, the inability to express emotions with words.

[22]Terry Real, *I Don't Want to Talk About It: Overcoming the Secret Legacy of Male Depression* (Scribner, 1998).

They describe us as cold or cynical. Wives complain that we don't open up and share what's going on in our hearts. They see us as closed off, more interested in distractions like sex, TV, or work. We can become masters of self-deception—the classic "I'm fine" when we are anything but.[23]

Generations of misguided methods of raising sons to not feel their negative emotions have produced men who lack the courage to open up about the real issues going on in their lives. Seeking to appear strong, they have instead become frail.

It's in moments of brokenness, pain, and loss that people need support and love most. But many men have been trained to stuff or handle these feelings on their own, and everyone is suffering the fallout.

We can do better. An emotionally healthy, vulnerable, honest man is a better husband, father, friend, and worker. And he feels vibrant in his ability to confess his feelings to God, while also relying on spiritual leaders and friends for support when he needs it. This is true for both spiritual fathers and sons.

God and Our Emotions

The Bible often uses rich language when talking about the emotions of God. We read about emotions of Anger (see Psalm 7:11), Compassion (see Deuteronomy 32:36; Judges 2:18), Love (see 1 John 4:8), Joy (see Isaiah 62:5; Jeremiah 32:41), Jealousy (see Exodus 20:5), and Hate (see Proverbs 6:16, Psalm 11:5).[24]
Just as God expresses Himself to us emotionally throughout the Bible, He expects us to do the same. We are image bearers of God, and therefore we have a rich emotional life as well.

We see this clearly in the life of Christ. Jesus was not an emotionless being or a robot. He wept and was overcome with sorrow. He expressed longing and desire for people. He had compassion for children and the poor, and He expressed anger when He saw injustice.

If God can express Himself in the full range of emotions, then why are men under the assumption that it is somehow against our nature to be emotional? On the contrary, our inability to express our emotions is a roadblock to our authentic existence—and brings with it an inability to fully express our faith.

Yes, our emotions are subject to sinful feelings of pride and other negative emotions. But the goal of our life should be to reclaim and sanctify our emotions, not reject them.

---

[23]In the movie *The Italian Job*, Donald Sutherland's character shares that "I'm fine" really means I'm "freaked out, insecure, neurotic, and emotional." An interesting commentary on modern men.
[24]God's emotions are not like human emotions, in that they are not uncontrollable reactions to unexpected situations. God's sovereignty means that He is never surprised, nor capricious, nor out of control.

Basic Feelings

In literature on the topic of emotions, you will often see a list of "primary" emotions. For instance, one might feel:

- Glad
- Sad
- Lonely
- Angry
- Afraid
- Hurt
- Ashamed

Our goal should be to reclaim and sanctify our emotions, not reject them.

You can think of them like primary colors. The primary colors are the basis for the full range of colors possible. A little kid with his crayons has a very different skillset than Van Gogh with his paint. The kid uses the basic colors from his crayon box, while Van Gogh mixes and shades his colors into a fuller range of expression. But they both are drawing with the same primary colors.

So it is with emotions. Emotionally vibrant, expressive people are not somehow tapped into a different set of emotions than the rest of us. They have the same basic emotions we do. What they have developed, though, is the ability to combine, shade, and nuance their emotional awareness to be able to communicate better.

That said, if a spiritual son struggles to express himself, it is best to start with these basics. "How are you feeling?" should be answered with, "I feel _____."

If the son is having trouble articulating strong feelings, an "Emotions Wheel" can be a helpful tool. An Emotions Wheel is basically a list of words to describe emotions. It arranges those words in sections, from basic emotions on the inside of the wheel, to more specific and distinct words on the outer rim. Someone feeling Sad, for instance, might express that more specifically as Lonely, Vulnerable, Despair, Guilty, Depressed or Hurt. And each of those has variations, such as the person who feels Lonely, might say they are feeling Isolated or Abandoned. An Emotions Wheel is included in Appendix I.

The goal here is twofold. First, helping a young man develop an emotional vocabulary will help him express himself more easily. As an illustration, imagine trying to describe a triangle to someone without the words "shape," "sides," "straight," or "three" in your vocabulary. That would be a frustrating exercise!

Second, once a man knows more specifically what he is feeling, he can address those feelings directly. Greater self-awareness leads to less frustration, which benefits both himself and those around him.

A note of caution here. Don't try to tell a spiritual son what he is feeling. As it relates to exploring and handling his emotions—whatever they may be—your role as a more experienced guide is to go along with him on his journey of self-discovery.

When we equip a younger man to decipher his own emotions, he is also better equipped to take positive action. A man who can reason with his guilty feelings can see what he must do: apologize to the son he yelled at. A man who feels lonely can be guided to find a time to reconnect and unplug from the demands of his life. Someone feeling fear often just needs to express that fear with someone he trusts.

Coaching a spiritual son, then, to have a healthy emotional life is mostly about redirecting him to recognize and articulate these basic emotions so that he can take the next right step.

Thinking vs. Feeling

A common habit when we try to describe our feelings is that we are actually describing our *thinking*. Plenty of us say "I feel" when what we are describing are thoughts or reflections. Consider the following statements from a son:

- I feel like my wife is wrong for being so annoyed when I go golfing.
- I feel angry thoughts about my boss lately.
- It feels like things are starting to improve.
- I feel that my kids are doing great with their schoolwork.

Only one of these statements is an emotional statement (the second one).

Part of the problem is how we speak. In the English language, we use the word "feel" to mean all kinds of things. But the problem for spiritual fathers is that, if we are not talking about emotions but *think* that we are, we run the risk of avoiding deeper issues.

Take the first example—*I feel like my wife is wrong for being so annoyed when I go golfing*. The statement isn't about his emotions at all. He just wants his wife to be fine with his golfing. He would have been more truthful if he said, "I think my wife should get over it." It's not an emotion; it's a thought: *I want to do this, and I want her to get off my back.*

The same is true of the final statement: *I feel my kids are doing great in school.* These are thoughts—good thoughts, but just thoughts. What the man feels is happy. He is happy that his kids are thriving. He feels proud of their accomplishments and a sense of joy since he is their father.

A good rule of thumb is to exchange the word "feel" with "think" and see if there is any difference in the meaning.

- I <u>think</u> that my wife is wrong for being so annoyed when I go golfing.
- I <u>think</u> angry thoughts about my boss lately.

- I <u>think</u> things are starting to improve.
- I <u>think</u> that my kids are doing great with their schoolwork.

Notice how clearly the difference stands out between the second statement and the others. Our thinking is important, but we don't want to use it to avoid our true emotions.

This is even more important when discussing conflict. Consider the following situation: Your spiritual son has conflict in the home. Whatever the issue, he and his wife are arguing. This is a prime place for you to lend an ear and help. After listening for a long while, you notice your son is diagnosing, reasoning, analyzing, and critiquing.

But in the case of marital strife, there are usually deep emotions at work. Deep emotions that he needs to face. It is crucial that you intentionally help your son shift from his reflections to his emotions:

Son: *I think she has a problem with my choices in life. She hates my job and doesn't respect me. She hates my friends, too.*

Father: *How does that make you feel?*

Son: *Well, I feel she is the one with the problem.*

Father: *I hear you, but my question was how that makes you feel.*

Son: *I feel that I'm doing my best and that she should lay off me and not be critical.*

Father: *Pause for a second. You are telling me how you think about it. And that's important, but this is some heavy stuff. I've been there and can help, but let's try and get to the feelings.*

Son: *What do you mean?*

Father: *Think about some of the more basic emotions. Would you say you feel surprised, bad, angry, fearful, disgusted, or sad? [Happy is probably not a candidate for this conversation.] You can pick more than one.*

Son: *Well, I feel bad, of course. But also, angry and sad. I want to have my wife's love and respect, and I'm afraid she doesn't feel that way about me.*

Notice how the father guides the son out of his mind and to his emotions. And by guiding the son to his emotions, he takes him to a much more vulnerable place.

From here, he can truly help his spiritual son. Rather than just arguing with logic to try to prove his case, the son can be encouraged to express his emotions or loneliness or fear to his wife—or, if need be, to seek professional help to guide the couple in their marriage.

The Problem of Anger

Many of us feel anger from time to time—or a version of it, such as frustration, grumpiness, or annoyance.

The truth is that anger is often a secondary emotion, not a primary one. One does not begin angry but rather experiences one of the other basic emotions first. For example, a man may find it hard to process that he feels sad and lonely, so that sadness and loneliness is allowed to fester until they eventually grow into anger.

Anger is dealt with in two ways as a spiritual father. First, you need to be a sounding board for a spiritual son's anger. With established trust and confidentiality, let him get it off his chest. Plenty of men have not let pent up anger out, and they need to express it in a way that is raw and vulnerable.

This is especially the case in family issues. A spiritual son may have struggles related to his wife, children, parents, or siblings. He needs the freedom to complain and let the words come out, no matter how rough they are. Listen carefully when he is expressing anger. You will learn a lot when he drops his guard, and pretense tends to go away in the heat of the moment.

But if you understand that anger is a secondary emotion, you have a second step for helping him deal with his anger. Once he has vented to you, guide him back to one of the primary emotions.

> *You're angry and you've let some of that out. I'm glad. But do you think that there is a more basic emotion at work here? Yes, you're angry with your wife for her coldness and distance. But you also mentioned feelings of loneliness and sadness. You miss her. You want her to be close to you. You are sad that things are not going well. And based on those emotions, you have a sense of anger that has grown.*
>
> *But if you go to her and tell her how angry you are, you'll only make things worse. However, if you go to her and say that you're sad and lonely and want to work on things... well, that's where you really are, deep down. And she's much more likely to respond well to those emotions than she is to your anger, which, frankly, probably frightens her.*

Notice in this example, you have allowed a secondary emotion to have its place, but you then take him to primary emotions. And by going to the primary emotions, you can hopefully start to make progress and provide him some real relief.

There are times when anger is appropriate and needs to be felt on its own. When someone experiences injustice or has been wronged, then anger is the natural, correct response. Similarly, if someone experiences the loss of a loved one, be aware that anger is a normal stage in the grief process.

But usually, anger is a mask hiding deep feelings, and we want to help men remove it. Your role as a spiritual father is to invite him to open up about those negative feelings that he may not yet have the skills to deal with on his own.

Guilt vs. Shame

One of the overriding and crippling emotions a man can feel is shame. Helping a spiritual son deal with his shame issues can be challenging for you and life-changing for him. But it's important to understand the differences between guilt and shame.

In our everyday speech, we often use guilt and shame interchangeably. However, in recent years, research into human emotions has found it necessary to distinguish between guilt and shame as we use them in English.

- Guilt: the sense of *responsibility* and *remorse* for my behavior.
- Shame: a sense of overall *unworthiness* in my being; a sense that I do not deserve to receive love.

The difference is profound. Guilt can be good when it's an honest admission of our actions or thoughts that are ungodly. In Genesis 3, Adam was guilty of disobeying God when he ate the forbidden fruit. We can experience guilt and repent and change from our behavior.

But shame is judgmental. It cuts us off from forgiveness. It was shame that drove Adam to hide from God, rather than confront his sin and ask for forgiveness. If a man struggles with an overall sense that he is unworthy and unlovable, then his entire identity is called into question.

Today, many men struggle with a deep sense of shame. Father wounds, broken relationships, a lack of close friends, past mistakes, and an overall sense of unworthiness have left men feeling lost.

A spiritual son may often describe a feeling of guilt when he is actually struggling with shame. Take the following statements as examples:

- I feel bad that I have to work so much, and I can't spend much time with my family. (Guilt)
- I fear that I am not a good father, and I'm just like my own father. (Shame)
- I am struggling with being rude to my wife when I'm tired or stressed. (Guilt)
- I am not cut out to be a good husband. (Shame)
- I'm having trouble with alcohol. I reach for it too often. (Guilt)
- I'm just not sure if I'm good at anything in life these days. (Shame)

Guilty feelings are about our *behavior*. We have done something, thought something, or felt something that we should not have. We feel convicted that we have wronged someone and God. We can use guilt as springboard into repentance because we can apologize for our behavior and work hard to not repeat those behaviors, with God's help.

We cannot do this from feelings of shame. Shame is the gnawing sense that we are unworthy—that something is flawed within us—not because of our sinful behavior, but because we are undeserving of love. Shame leaves us feeling that even the good things in our life are there by mistake, and the other shoe will drop at any time. It's imposter syndrome on steroids.

Guilt and shame look and sound the same to the untrained ear. But they require radically different approaches from a spiritual father. Put simply, a spiritual son can be called out for guilty behavior, and encouraged to stop the behavior that creates guilt. We can support them as an accountability partner to repent and accept God's forgiveness.

But a man dealing with shame is starved for affirmation and trust. A man dealing with shame needs the loving and gentle kindness of a father. Remind him of who He is in Christ. He needs to be told that he is loved. And he needs to be reminded often that he should not have guilty feelings about his need for love.

> *Shame is the gnawing sense that we are unworthy—that something is flawed within us—not because of our sinful behavior, but because we are undeserving of love.*

Feelings Exercise

If you or your spiritual son realize you need to develop a stronger grasp on your emotions, it can be helpful to follow an exercise.

Here's how it works—each day of the week, fill out the following set of questions in a journal.

Explain a Situation
What happened today that impacted your emotions more strongly than what you'd encounter normally?
Example: *My wife and I got into an argument over the kids.*

Who was involved?
Example: *My wife and I, but our kids heard us arguing.*

Why did this happen?
Example: *I was frustrated about her parenting, and it just came out quickly and started a fight.*

Were there any other factors that provoked this?

Example: *I was tired from work and didn't sleep well the night before. I was grumpy.*

Write a Feeling Statement

Using the basic emotional list above, fill out the following.

Example: *I feel sad and surprised by the argument we had and the anger that came out.*

Reframe the Emotion

Did you do anything sinful during this emotional situation?

Example: *Yes, I spoke rudely to my wife during the argument. And I spoke this way in front of the kids.*

Were your feelings justified?

Example: *Although my concern was justified, I feel I did not express it in a healthy way.*

Was there a deeper emotion that may have been driving you?

Example: *Yes, I was afraid that her parenting would have a negative impact on our children. But I reached for anger to express it instead of fear.*

Look Forward

Is there anyone you need to repent to or make amends?

Example: *I need to apologize to my wife and kids.*

Once you've made amends, how will you express your emotions?

Example: *I will open up to my wife that I am afraid of what is happening.*

What will it take for you to feel better?

Example: *If I ask forgiveness and have an honest conversation with my wife, I will feel better.*

Pray

How can I bring this to God for help?

Write out a prayer, including, for example:

- *Confession and repentance.*
- *Gratitude to God for opening your eyes to the issues.*
- *Asking Him for help in making amends.*
- *Asking Him to use this to help you grow in your faith.*

This exercise may feel rote or simplistic but think of it like going to the gym. Repetition will gradually make emotions easier to recognize and deal with in a healthy, godly way.

A Spiritual Father and Son Story –
Chapter Eight: Sean's Bad Day

When Frank and Sean grabbed dinner after work one day, Frank could tell right away something was bothering him, so he asked.

"It's my boss. He's an %&*#@!"

Well, that was an interesting start to their conversation! Sean talked about how they were working on a big project at work and the deadline was fast approaching. Things had not been going smoothly.

"Did something happen?" Frank asked.

"I just feel like the guy doesn't appreciate a single thing I do. I've put in extra time and effort, stayed late, helped other people, and then he gets mad at me and says I have an attitude. He wants an attitude? I'll show him an attitude!"

"Alright, Sean. Let's slow down a little and talk it through. The project is behind, you're putting in a lot of extra effort, and your boss is on your back, right? How does that make you feel?"

"It ticks me off!" Sean exclaimed.

"So, it makes you angry. Why?"

"What do you mean why? Because I'm being treated unfairly!"

"I get it. I've been there before at my past job, and it made me angry, too. But I'm wondering what other emotions you might be feeling, aside from the anger?"

With some coaxing, Sean thought about it and shared that he was surprised that his extra effort wasn't being appreciated; fearful that he might lose his job, or at least that the problems would reflect poorly on his next evaluation; and a little guilty because he had made a few honest mistakes that had cost the team some time.

As they continued to talk, he also admitted that his frustration had caused him to speak sharply to his coworkers, as well as to his boss. In retrospect, he had not behaved well, even though his coworkers understood where he was coming from and agreed with his points.

After he and Frank talked through some possible next steps, Sean decided to apologize to his coworkers and boss, and they accepted. He also requested a meeting to sit down with his boss and discuss the project.

Sean also noticed his work stress had been overflowing to his time at home with his wife, causing him to act distant. He called Frank at their regularly scheduled time on Wednesday morning and shared his realization.

After Frank asked him some key questions to help him get down to the emotions behind his actions, Sean saw that he'd been afraid to appear weak or incompetent in front of his wife. Yet, once he had distanced himself, he also felt lonely because he wasn't talking to her about what he was going through. With Frank's encouragement, Sean decided to talk to his wife about his problems at work, and he also planned to share the feelings he was experiencing.

On Thursday, when Frank received Sean's daily text check-in, Sean sheepishly reported that his wife had been very encouraging and supportive. He felt so much more at ease and happy. He realized his emotions had been valid, but he had been handling them in ways that made things worse, not better. All it had taken for things to start improving was bringing them to the surface.

Takeaways

- Men aren't born emotionally closed off; these are learned behaviors, and they can be unlearned.

- The difficulty in expressing our feelings comes with harder emotions that require vulnerability.

- An inability to express our emotions brings with it an inability to fully express our faith.

- The seven primary emotions are happiness, pride, sadness, loneliness, fear, guilt, and surprise.

- Coaching a spiritual son to have a healthy emotional life is mostly about redirecting him to recognize and articulate his basic emotions so that he can take the next right step.

- It is crucial to intentionally help a spiritual son shift from his reflections and thoughts to his emotions.

- Anger is a secondary emotion. A spiritual father can be a safe place for a man to vent his anger, but then he can help guide him to the deeper emotions behind it.

- Guilt and shame look and sound the same to the untrained ear. But they require radically different approaches from a spiritual father.

Discussion

1) Do you struggle to express or discuss emotions? What is one thing you can do this week to help you grow in this area?

2) What are some things that make you feel deeply?

3) Describe a time when you felt angry. What was the primary emotion underneath it?

4) Spend a few minutes reviewing the Emotions Wheel appendix. Think of a time of high emotion in the past week or so and use the Wheel to tell the group about it.

5) Where do you struggle with shame in your life?

Prayer

Take a few minutes and share prayer requests around the group in the following areas: family, work, social, and personal.

Pray for the Holy Spirit to reveal to each of you your own emotions and equip you to help a spiritual son discover theirs as well. Pray over the areas of your lives that are causing any of you to feel difficult emotions.

Continue to pray that God would direct you to the right person on your list of potential spiritual sons.

Notes

SKILLS FOR MENTORING

CHAPTER **9**

ACTIVE-LISTENING TECHNIQUES

The world today is moving at such a frenetic pace that we rarely stop to listen to each other.

We've all been in conversations with someone we felt wasn't listening. Their body language appears jittery. They keep looking at their watch or at other people around them. They nod and say, "Mmhmm." But we feel like they're not really present.

Few of us would do this on purpose to a spiritual son, but the truth is, being a good listener is a skill. While it may sound easy—*just listen to your spiritual son*—the skills presented in this chapter require focus and some practice.

Listening Is Fathering

Listening is an act of trust and acceptance—two qualities that are vital to a close father-son relationship.

The Bible repeatedly speaks of God as a Father who listens to His children:

> *Such is God's heart that even in all his omnipotent glory, He still makes time to listen to His children.*

> *And this is the confidence that we have toward him, that if we ask anything according to his will he hears us. And if we know that he hears us in whatever we ask, we know that we have the requests that we have asked of him.* (1 John 5:14-15)

> *The eyes of the Lord are toward the righteous and his ears toward their cry.* (Psalm 34:15)

> *Then you will call upon me and come and pray to me, and I will hear you.* (Jeremiah 29:12)

Such is God's heart that even in all His omnipotent glory, He still makes time to listen to His children.

If we are to be spiritual fathers to young men as God is our heavenly Father, we must be listeners. To listen is to love. And to listen, therefore, is to love another as Christ loves us.

You may have little practice listening to a son, and it's likely they have little experience speaking openly with a father. But as Christian men, our ability to listen is held in high regard in the Bible. For example, James encourages Christians to "be quick to listen, slow to speak and slow to become angry" (see James 1:19). Taken in context, the word "anger" here also implies becoming overly animated, opinionated, or pushy.

> *Becoming skilled at listening reflects our maturity in Christ, and it honors our son's genuine need to be heard by a father figure.*

As spiritual fathers, we want to be *unwilling* to interrupt others with our opinions. Giving someone else the space to speak is more important.

Becoming skilled at listening reflects our maturity in Christ, and it honors a spiritual son's genuine need to be heard by a father figure.

Resisting the Urge to Speak

Be sure to leave time and space when you're together for your son to let anything out that might be bottled up—the good, the bad, and the ugly. When he feels comfortable doing this, be prepared that it may come out in a tidal wave. Being able to listen well and ask the right questions in these moments will be legitimately therapeutic to him.

If he's having trouble in his marriage, for example, it's likely he already knows intellectually most of the advice that people would offer him. What he needs is the space to be able to vent—and a spiritual father who can then steer him to the emotions at play in his pain, as discussed in the previous chapter. That takes an enormous amount of verbal processing to achieve.

What is *not* needed is for the conversation to go like this:

Father: *So how are things in your marriage lately?*

Son: *Eh, it's been rough for us.*

Father: *How so?*

Son: *Well, we just fight all the time, and it's really annoying.*

Father: *You know, what you need is...*

Here, the spiritual father has not really heard the spiritual son. He has not probed the problem, nor has he allowed him to find his own way to the bottom of his emotions. Instead, the father here is quick to speak, striving to fix the son rather than love him. It's unhelpful.

Older men have often accrued a lot of life experience, and it can be tempting for us to launch into what we think will fix things.

You have valuable life experience and want to give good counsel. But quickly jumping into advice-giving mode short-circuits the point you want to make. Rather than feeling he's learned something helpful, he experiences it as getting cut off and told what to do.

Your advice can be a healthy part of a son's life. But you want your advice to be timely and fruitful. If your natural instincts are to dominate a conversation or tell others how to solve their problems, then the son will not be well served.

Simply listening is also a good way to show that you care about and empathize with a spiritual son's perspective. Many young men today are allergic to older men who act like know-it-alls. Chalk it up to them growing up with no fathers or bad fathers, but they tend to be weary of older men asserting their opinions. And what they see on social media from older men hasn't helped.

> *There will be a time and place for sharing your opinions and advice. But first and foremost, as you're building the relationship, be a listener.*

Again, there will be a time and place for sharing your opinions and advice. But first and foremost, as you're building the relationship, be a listener. There is great power in the phrase, *I'm here if you need to talk.*

If the son is going through something difficult, he may not have another outlet for being truly heard. Yes, he may have plenty of friends, likes, and followers, but heart emojis and comments of "thoughts and prayers" hardly soothe a hurting spirit that craves intimacy with another human being.

It is our ability to listen well that will shape the relationship as something healthy, authentic, and transformative in his life.

The Character of a Listener

Regularly demonstrating the simple art of listening is part of what it means to live a godly life. Many of the character traits that mark a good listener are the same traits that mark a mature Christian—

A listening father is HUMBLE.

The Bible holds out humility as one of the highest aims of the Christian life. It starts with our place before the cross—broken and sinful, and yet, redeemed and accepted. When we see that we live under grace, we are humbled and can more freely extend grace to others.

The Bible tells us that those who have humility have wisdom (see Proverbs 11:2). Paul tells us to be completely humble (see Ephesians 4:2) and to do nothing out of selfish ambition or vain conceit (see Philippians 2:3). In fact, Paul never stops encouraging Christians to slow down, hold our tongues, and be humble.

Again, being humble does not mean that our opinions or advice are worthless. But rather it means we hold lightly the need to offer our advice before we have explored others' needs.

> *Being humble means we hold lightly the need to offer advice before we have explored others' needs.*

A listening spiritual father is PATIENT.

Proverbs tells us that those with patience also have great wisdom and understanding (see Proverbs 14:29). And Paul shows us that love itself is, at its heart, an act of patience (see 1 Corinthians 13:4).

Demonstrating patience in our own lives is often a struggle, but it can be equally as difficult when dealing with a spiritual son. We may recognize some of the same patterns and sins and want better for them. But to be patient listeners is to let a son speak and share without trying to hustle them along.

A listening father is GENTLE.

Gentleness is a byproduct of the Holy Spirit's work in our lives that is crucial to our roles as spiritual fathers. The Proverbs talk about the power of a gentle response during tense conversations (see Proverbs 15:1), and Paul writes that God's chosen people should clothe themselves in it (see Colossians 3:12).

In normal discussions about the points of daily life, the need for gentleness may be less pronounced. However, when a spiritual son is facing a crisis, anxiety, or pain, the need for you to be gentle is critical.

A listening father is PURPOSEFUL.

True, authentic listening is not a matter of just waiting for your turn to talk. It's active and purposeful. Active listeners strive to remember details or even take notes so they can reflect on them later.

A skilled spiritual father asks himself:

- Am I understanding what he is going through?
- Do I get the sense that something deeper is going on?
- How is his body language and mood? Is he reaching for anger or other emotions, too?
- How can I help without trying to "fix" everything for him?

> *True, authentic listening is not a matter of just waiting for your turn to talk. It's active and purposeful.*

It can help to journal your conversations with a spiritual son so you can reflect on what you heard, pray for him, and consider how you can serve and love him better.

A listening father is SPIRITUAL.

Remember that the Holy Spirit is present when you meet with your spiritual son. This should be a source of comfort and confidence, but also of humility and restraint. Paul writes in Galatians that the fruit of the Spirit is love, joy, peace, patience, kindness, goodness, faithfulness, gentleness, and self-control (see 5:22-23). This fruit is not cultivated by trying to be more loving or patient or gentle, but by seeking to know God more intimately.

Do not neglect your own walk with God. Your time in the Word, in prayer, in worship, and in fellowship with like-minded brothers will prepare and equip you for your role as a spiritual father.

And do not rely on your own wisdom and experience. When possible and appropriate, point your spiritual son to the truth of Scripture, pray with and for him, and help him trust in the saving grace of Christ.

Types of Listening

Two aspects of listening are important for spiritual fathers in particular: listening for information and listening for compassion.

Listening for Information

You are always listening for information when you're with a spiritual son, taking in what he says and how it all fits together. You are trying to remember the names of his wife and kids, his job, his stress points—anything and everything you can.

This is where most fathers feel comfortable. Since it is primarily the act of taking in information, it feels easier and more natural—two men swapping stories.

This form of listening, of course, is important. You do need to know things about your spiritual son. But there is a deeper level of listening that we also must get to.

Listening for Compassion

This is sometimes called *therapeutic listening*, and it can be a challenge for some men. It's less about receiving information and more about processing.

Women tend to instinctively be better at this form of listening. They can engage in long conversations and not necessarily be focused on sharing information. Instead, they are sharing their experiences, processing emotions, and expressing everything on their minds.

Often, they don't expect a lot of pushback or solutions to be offered. They just want their friends to listen and empathize.

While men don't have to converse in the same ways as women, we should be able to talk freely with someone and know we've been heard. It may look like venting, getting something off your chest, or saying what you really think without fear of judgment or rebuke. But we need friends we can complain to and confide in. And we need to *be* that friend to others, offering a compassionate, confidential ear—especially to spiritual sons.

Take, for example, a young man who has just been let go from his job without warning. He calls his spiritual father on his way home from what used to be his office, a tornado of emotions and thoughts. He's angry, he's sad, he feels rejected, and he's fearful about how he's going to survive.

The spiritual father can step in and give him the freedom to vent and process it all. He may be the only person to whom he can release his emotions. This is compassionate listening.

The point is not that there are enough words to fix his situation. The point is that he has the freedom to be heard. His spiritual father simply has to say, "I'm so sorry, and I wish I had a quick way to fix it. Say whatever you need to and be as raw as you want."

The Mechanics of Active Listening

If you want to become a better listener, here are four things to be mindful of when your spiritual son is talking:

> *Put your phone away, make eye contact, lean forward, and focus.*

Body Language
Body language is both the easiest thing to ignore and the easiest to fix! The basics are simple: Put your phone away, make eye contact, lean forward, and focus.

In addition, never underestimate the value of a smile, head nod, or other expression of connection.

Repetition and Clarification
Have you ever played the game Telephone? You think you're communicating one thing to the person next to you, only to realize they heard something much different. The same can happen in our conversations.

One skill you can practice to combat these kinds of misunderstandings is to ask questions and then repeat back what you heard. The purpose of this is to confirm that you understood.

A phrase you can use is, "What I hear you saying is…"

Alternatively, you can use the phrase, "Tell me more about that." This is helpful when you feel like you aren't quite understanding what he is trying to tell you.

Keep asking those types of questions until you are sure you have a good grasp on what he's telling you. You can also summarize it using the salient points from his responses. Be sure that he agrees with you, and if he alters your clarification, be sure to acknowledge the change.

Normalizing vs. Minimizing

If something is bothering the spiritual son enough for him to bring it up, it is a big deal to him. Be careful not to diminish or downplay what he has said. If your spiritual son has unburdened himself about a problem with his boss, a conflict with a roommate, or pulling another all-nighter with the new baby, it is inappropriate to respond in ways that suggest his concerns are no big deal.

With age and experience comes a mature perspective that he may not have yet. But never minimize his experience or his feelings. Whether the matter on his plate is relatively light or very heavy, it is a privilege to enter into it by humbly letting him talk and listening with compassion.

Instead, let him know that others deal with the same frustrations, disappointments, and difficulties he does. Normalizing helps him realize he is not alone. Others have faced the same challenges and overcome them—and so can he.

Relate

Being able to relate to a young man's situation or experience is important. When a spiritual son is telling you what's going on in his life, and the natural flow points to you responding, avoid "you" statements and turn them into "I" statements. In other words, do everything you can to relate to his situation.

Take these two examples of a conversation—

Son: *I'm really stressed out at home.*

Father: *Why is that?*

Son: *Well, with the kids being so young, my wife and I feel like our heads are under water. We barely have time to think.*

Father: *That's not fun. What do you think would help?*

Son: *I'm not sure.*

Father: *You should get a sitter so you can do a regular date night.*

In many ways, this is a fine conversation. The father is expressing interest in the son's situation and asking questions. He hasn't fallen into the trap of giving advice immediately, which is good.

But notice that he keeps a distance by talking to his son about his problem. The father is not entering into the conversation with compassion. Each comment or question involves a "you" statement to the son.

Now see the difference when you enter in with your son and use relatability—

Son: *I'm really stressed out at home.*

Father: *I'm so sorry you feel that way. What's going on that is causing the stress?*

Son: *Well, with the kids being so young, my wife and I feel like our heads are under water. We barely have time to think.*

Father: *Oh man! That's not fun. I can totally relate. My wife and I went through that quite a few times with the kids where we felt overwhelmed. How can I help?*

Son: *Thanks. How did you guys deal with it?*

Father: *Well, it wasn't easy, and I had a lot of fights with my wife out of exhaustion. I'm sure you guys are maybe doing the same. In our case, we found having scheduled date nights was a big help—at least one night a week where we could just be us without the kids. We looked forward to it every week. It was an expense, but it was worth it.*

The father has a desire to relate and connect with his son's situation. He uses "I" statements, relating his own experience to what the son is going through. He lets him know implicitly that he knows the situation personally.

And only once he's asked, does he offer advice by sharing his experience.

Asking Helpful Questions

In some cases, spiritual sons may have a hard time clarifying their thoughts or articulating their emotions and needs. They may be all over the map or fall into silence.

Rather than moving on from a subject he is clearly still concerned about, his spiritual father can help him by being ready with a few thoughtful, open-ended questions.

These questions are for when he's stuck or at a loss for words—

- How are you feeling about that?
- You said _____, can you say more about that?
- What do you think you need or want in this situation right now?
- What would help right now?
- Have you talked to anyone else about this? What did they say?

Note that the questions are all designed to gently help him reflect further. The goal is not to lead him to a given answer, but simply probing how he really feels. Maybe he just needs to vent, or maybe it's a serious problem that needs some reflection or action. But it is up to the spiritual son to build self-awareness about what he feels and wants. And asking good questions is very helpful.

Topics to Avoid

It's worth noting a few issues that can occur when older and younger men intersect. The most common one is older men's propensity to bring up politics or "culture war" topics, unsolicited.

> *There may be trends or fads that you, as an older man, find silly or strange.*

Many young men are largely turned off by the current state of American politics. This is more of a social issue than a matter of aptitude or a lack of concern. They may have grown up watching their families argue and divide over these issues—and they are aware of how often a preferred political party becomes a deity for some people.

The basic rule is only discuss politics if the spiritual son says he finds the subject interesting. And then do so sparingly and carefully.[25]

The key is to avoid any sense that you have an agenda with your spiritual son.

The same is true when it comes to trends or fads that you, as an older man, find silly or strange. We want to avoid the impression that we are curmudgeonly old men who find younger men strange. A spiritual son may be into all sorts of things you don't relate to—video games, popular media, social media apps, disc golf, fashion choices, music preferences, etc.

These are all non-essential matters. Suspend your judgment and welcome your differences.

> *In nonessential matters, suspend your judgment and welcome your differences.*

Once the relationship is well established, one of those differences could even become an inside joke between the two of you! But never allow them to create a sense of division.

A Spiritual Father and Son Story –
Chapter Nine: Know-It-All Frank

As Frank was talking to his group at their monthly meeting, they began to reminisce about some of the mistakes they had made early on.

Frank cringed when he remembered his second time getting lunch with Sean. "I remember getting to the end of the meeting and feeling like it had gone really great! Sean had brought up three different issues he was struggling with, and boy, I had great advice for him. I solved each of his problems in 15 minutes," he said, sarcastically.

---

[25]The same might be said about "pet theologies." Unless you and your spiritual son are trained theologians—possible, but unlikely—getting into the finer points of the latest YouTube preacher with a new spin on ancient truths is unlikely to be fruitful. If your spiritual son has gotten pulled down a theological rabbit hole that you feel ill-equipped to handle, consult your pastor.

"I remember that, too," chuckled Joe, one of the other spiritual fathers. "Do you remember how we responded when you told us that?"

"Oooooh, yeah, that's right," said Frank. "You guys made it clear I had come across as a know-it-all. In fact, I'm pretty sure one of you actually said, 'Okay, boomer.'" They all laughed.

"So, what ever happened with that?" asked Pete, a new member of their group.

"Well," recalled Frank, "In the next meeting we had, I apologized right up front. I told him I realized I had been more interested in solving his problems at our previous meeting than really listening and getting to know him, and I asked for his forgiveness."

"You said that?!" Pete looked stunned. "What did he say?"

"At first, his face looked a little like yours right now! But then he kind of acknowledged that he had felt that way, too. Now I'm much better at listening to Sean before I respond. In fact, a lot of the time he needs me to encourage him to keep talking. So, I ask open questions to help him process whatever is on his mind. If I'm not sure I heard something correctly, I just summarize it, and he clarifies before continuing. It took a lot of practice on my end, but our conversations are so much deeper and there are fewer misunderstandings."

Frank paused and grinned. "Want to know what the best part is, though? Half the time I don't ever give any advice at all. He solves his own problems just by talking it out with me. And I look like a genius!"

Takeaways

- Listening skills require focus and practice to develop.

- The Bible repeatedly speaks of God as a Father who listens to His children.

- Allowing someone to open up and share their life with us communicates the simple truth: *you matter, and I care about your life.*

- A listening father is humble, patient, gentle, and purposeful.

- We must know how to listen for both information and compassion.

- When your spiritual son is sharing something with you, be mindful of your body language, use repetition and clarification, never minimize his concerns, and relate to him.

- Asking thoughtful, open questions can help someone process their thoughts and emotions.

- Be sure to clarify and confirm.

- Never let your differences on the non-essentials divide you.

Discussion

1) Are there any situations where you are prone to talk too much and listen too little?

2) Which of the techniques in this chapter feels the most difficult to you?

3) What topics have caused division in a discipleship relationship for you before?

4) Practice listening to each other in five-minute intervals, where one person is in the role of talker and the other is in the role of listener.

Prayer

Take a few minutes and share prayer requests around the group in the following areas: family, work, social, and personal.

Pray that God would help you listen well to each other within your small group, as well as to your spiritual sons in the days ahead.

Notes

ENCOURAGEMENT

It is not a sign of weakness for men to long for praise from a father. In fact, we are all wired to give and receive praise. All throughout the Bible, God Himself dotes on his children as a loving Father.

In this example of a father's love from the book of Proverbs, we see the impact of his encouragement and guidance on his son:

> *I will guide you in the way of wisdom and I will lead you in upright paths.*
> *When you walk, your steps will not be hampered, and when you run, you*
> *will not stumble.* (Proverbs 4:11-12, NET)

Few things have the power to impact us as much as the gifts of praise and encouragement. They will be vital to your spiritual father-son relationship.

The Basics of Encouraging

Men can tend to be long on critique and lean on encouragement. But in your role as a spiritual father to a younger man, encouragement should make up the bulk of your interactions.

Consider, again, the biblical discipleship example of Paul and Timothy. Paul describes his role in Timothy's life as being a man who will "remind you to help God's gift grow, just as a small spark grows into a fire" (see 2 Timothy 1:6, NIrV).

In fact, throughout his ministry, Paul is quick with his praise and support of those in his care. Of course, he rebukes as well, but only in the worst of circumstances—when someone is living in open sin, refusing to listen to God's word, and then presenting those as good things in the church. Overall, Paul is slow to anger and slow to criticize. And to his disciples, he is gentle, longsuffering, and kind. He encourages and uplifts them with his words.

You need to assume in all circumstances that a spiritual son is hungry for encouragement and praise, and then be lavish with it—even if it feels awkward. Early in your relationship with a spiritual son, encourage him regularly. If you wait or hesitate to encourage him, you run the risk of missing out on perhaps the most important part of the role of a spiritual father.

3 Important Times to Praise

Praising s spiritual son should happen as often
as possible, but here are three times when it's
particularly important:

1) Praise him directly when you notice growth.

When we recognize a character flaw in ourselves, we
may struggle mightily to correct it. We see the failures
and regret our behavior. We also tend to be slow to
see growth. This is just a fact of life.

> *Encourage early in the relationship and often. If you wait or hesitate to encourage him, you run the risk of missing out on perhaps the most important part of your role as a spiritual father.*

Therefore, it's extremely helpful to tell a spiritual
son when you notice growth in certain areas of his
life. For example, if he is struggling with his attitude
and anger—either at home or work or just in
general—you may notice after a season that he seems
to have more gratitude. When you do, communicate it directly to him:

> *I have watched you struggle with contentment and patience—and how it has
> often made you angry—but I want you to know I see a real change in you.
> You're telling me how you've learned to calm down and see the big picture.
> This is God working in your heart and mind. Keep it up!*

2) Praise him in front of others.

When you introduce him to someone—your wife, or a friend, for example—say
to the other person in front of your spiritual son how much you enjoy hanging out
with him.

Too many men carry the weight of feeling like they are a disappointment to
their real father. Be a spiritual father, then, who likes him and is proud of him. Say
positive things about him to others, openly and sincerely. For example:

> *I want to introduce you to my friend, _____. We've gotten to spend a lot
> of time together over the past several months, and I consider him like a son
> or younger brother. He's a great dad to two kids and works hard in his career.
> I'm really proud of him.*

Will he be a little embarrassed? Probably! But he will also feel affirmed and
encouraged, even if it is a little uncomfortable.

3) Praise him during milestones.

As the relationship grows, it's important that you do whatever you can to show up
for your spiritual son during milestones in his life, such as the birth of a new baby, a
promotion at work or start of a new job, a child's baptism, or his birthday.

These are pivotal moments to celebrate with him, and you should see them as opportunities to take extra steps to uplift him, as a loving father would. You might even write him a letter or get him a meaningful card. For example:

> *I wanted to write you a quick note on the anniversary of your wedding to Sarah. I see you striving to be a good husband to her—the kind of man she deserves. I know you didn't have a good example of this growing up, but in God's mercy, I see you doing what God asks of us as men: to love our wife as Christ loves the church. So today, enjoy your anniversary! I'm proud of you.*

But remember that some milestones are unwanted and heartbreaking, such as going through a divorce, getting fired from a job, or finding out your teenager is drinking or having sex. When it comes to difficult milestones, your praise and encouragement will be more important than ever, as you serve as a steady shoulder to lean on.

Encouraging Good Character

We should be quick to encourage men in their overall character. These are, in part, the sort of encouragements we find in Proverbs—a father telling his son to stay the course, stand tall, and do the right thing.

Accountability

We are all prone to pride and ego. But owning our mistakes and holding ourselves accountable to a higher standard is one of the primary virtues of a man.

> *Make it clear that taking responsibility and repenting of our sin is a sign of strength, not weakness.*

Encourage your spiritual son in this area when needed. Make it clear that taking responsibility and repenting of our sin is a sign of *strength*, not weakness.

Talk with him about specific areas where men often need accountability, sharing some of your own areas. Ask concrete questions and offer encouragement—*without judgement*—in areas where he admits he has failed. Be generous with your encouragement and acknowledge when he shows progress.

But beware: accountability outside of trust is legalism. And trust takes time to build. The accountability you offer at first must be light, helpful, and invited.

Accountability is also a two-way street. Invite your spiritual son to provide accountability in areas of your life where you struggle as well. For example, if you tend to work late too often, invite him to ask you about how often you've been home on time lately. As you open up and involve him in discussions about your own sin and struggles, as well as your repentance and process of growth, you are modeling how he can freely do this with you as well.

Maturity

Years or decades are lost for men who have never been encouraged to maturity, leaving many of them stuck in adolescence.

If this happens to be the case for your spiritual son, his lack of maturity should never be something to mock or tease. Instead, you can acknowledge the struggle while still being encouraging.

Let your spiritual son know that maturity is as much about the good things we choose to do as it is about the detrimental things we avoid. Maturity is a pattern of life that involves a lot of sacrifice and putting our own wants to the side for a greater good (see Ephesians 5:25). Examples to use might include choosing to play with your kids at the end of a draining day, choosing to save money by bringing your lunch to work, or choosing to log off devices at a certain time each evening.

Again, Paul consistently encourages his disciples in maturity: Leave the old behind. Strive for the better things of God. Grow in God's grace in a way that makes the distractions of our already distracted world seem pale in comparison.[26]

Be deliberate about recognizing when he displays character traits that show maturity, such as a strong work ethic, sense of humility, or act of sacrifice.

Never attempt to encourage maturity with a whip. Embarrassing or shaming someone over areas of immaturity isn't fruitful. Rather, hold space for him to be honest about his life patterns, and then gently encourage him to consider better ones.

Note that there might be a strong generational gap in this area, depending on the age of the man you're building a relationship with. Men born before 1980 married younger, had children younger, and started their careers not long after college. Life for the average man in his 20s today looks very different than it did for the average man in his 20s when you were first navigating adulthood.

If he tells you he feels aimless or you notice he seems heavily distracted by entertainment, media, or other forms of escapism, your encouragement and guidance are crucial. For example:

> *Listen, man. I know it's a lot of fun to focus on a hobby. For me, I love it when I get the chance to play a round of golf. But it can be tempting to get lost in all kinds of distractions. This isn't a judgement; it's just that I speak from experience when I say the more you can get a handle on how much time you spend on these things, the better.*

> *It seems fun now, but the opportunity cost isn't worth it.*

> *You know, it's really the goal of our lives in Christ to grow in maturity and sacrifice. But ironically, that's when life gets good. Maturity looks good on a man.*

---

[26]2 Corinthians 5:17 and Philippians 3:13-14 are great verses to memorize as reminders of this.

Encouraging Men in Practical Matters

Some of you have gained a lot of life experience in practical skills that are invaluable to younger men. Maybe you're good at doing work around the house or in the yard, running a business, or parenting kids with very different personalities, for example.

> *Practical issues provide a better starting point early in the relationship.*

You also by now probably have some regrets in life—maybe you wish you had saved for retirement sooner, had known how to wisely buy a house, or understood the importance of an annual physical. These experiences, too, are invaluable.

Although spiritual matters and character are the core areas of focus for spiritual fathering, we should see our role as moving beyond these areas to include practical everyday issues of life. In fact, often these practical issues provide a better starting point early in the relationship.

Family Life

If your spiritual son is married, encourage him by verbally noticing areas where he is loving his wife well. This comes more naturally when there are no big issues in the marriage, but even if they're in a difficult season, you can be a source of encouragement and help build his confidence.

At the right time, you can also include practical advice with your encouragement—tips such as doing more around the house, planning a date night, leaving a love note for his wife in the morning before work, etc.

If he notices his wife has a lot on her plate, for example, but isn't sure where to jump in, offer to teach him how to cook a few go-to meals if he's never had the opportunity, so he can make dinner a couple nights a week. Or, if he doesn't feel like he's good at expressing himself through writing, ask if he'd like help or suggest a good card store. In addition to helpful tips, this is one of those areas where some of those regrets or hard-earned lessons should be shared openly and honestly.

If your spiritual son is a dad, be a voice of encouragement and a source of wisdom as he navigates fatherhood.

Work, stress, hobbies—all kinds of things tend to distract us from this important role. But as many of us know, childhood is over in the blink of an eye. Encourage him to focus on and find joy in his kids while they are young. His presence in their lives is a gift only he can give them.

If you notice his priorities are off, gently urge him to reorder things by asking good questions and sharing any regrets you have related to when you had young children. Using your own experiences, explain why it will matter to him later that the Little League games and dance recitals came before another late night at work or disc golf with the guys.

And if he has a unique situation that presents further challenges to him, such as a child with special needs, a chronic illness, or a severe behavioral problem, look for ways to encourage him by actively serving him in helpful ways.

Health

There's nothing manly or admirable about overworking yourself into poor health, or about passively sinking into it.

The ways in which we take care of themselves—food, exercise, sleep, rest—impact not only our physical health, but also our mental and spiritual wellbeing.

Encourage the young man you're meeting with to continue or start healthy habits. For example, if he complains of exhaustion from burning the candle at both ends, encourage him to take a day off, plan a vacation, or go to sleep at a regular time.

This is also an area where you might be able to take a more active approach. If he wants to lose weight, you could ask if he wants to start meeting up at the gym twice a week before work. Or if he complains he's been "eating like crap," offer to help him make a grocery list and ask how he is doing with making better choices.

Again, use your own stories to help him realize his limitations and create better rhythms.

DIY and Home Repair

It's common for young men to spend their early adult years living in dorm rooms, apartments, or their parents' house. As a result, if they go on to buy a house, it's challenging to handle basic home projects.

Even young men who have been homeowners for a long time often have a pile of "honey do" lists stacked up, and little time to complete them.

> *Most older men are surprised at how may skills younger men wish they could learn.*

If you are talented—or even competent—in these areas, this is a great opportunity to get shoulder to shoulder with a spiritual son. Offer to help him tackle a project over the weekend or ask him over to your home to learn a few specific skills. Working on a project together helps create a stronger bond, as you encourage him along the way.

It's empowering for a man to learn how to take care of his own property, whether it's his home, his yard, or a vehicle. Most older men are surprised at how many skills younger men wish they could learn. This is a natural way to grow a spiritual father-son relationship.

Work

Young men have a myriad of questions about work-related issues. They may be related to a problem with a coworker, unethical business practices, negotiating pay, answering interview questions, communication issues with a boss, or career advancement.

Work is a great source of connection with your son. Even if you don't share similar career paths or skillsets, you can still be a source of encouragement and a listening ear.

The fact is you have many more years of experience navigating hard things like disappointment on the job, downsizing, and failing at a project. Share those experiences and encourage him to learn from your hard-earned lessons.

Additionally, be alert for tangible things you might be able to guide him through, such as writing his resume or what to wear to a job interview.

Finances

Don't assume that a young man already knows how to manage his finances. He may still be working on the basics, like making and sticking to a budget. Then of course, there are plenty of other matters, like saving for a home or other big goal, investing, paying down debt, etc.

Feel free to ask about these matters, as conversation leads and as your relationship develops, and encourage healthy habits.

If you struggle with certain areas of your finances, you may be wondering how helpful you can really be to him. But you probably have more advice and encouragement to offer in this area than you think, having had more time in the saddle.

If, on the other hand, you know you are well equipped to offer nuanced financial advice, you should feel free to do so. But it may be helpful to maintain a good boundary here, as you are not his financial advisor. That said, perhaps you can point him to one.

No matter how competent you are when it comes to money, you can encourage responsibility and stewardship. Younger men tend to be vulnerable to bad financial habits—perhaps some you fell into yourself. Use your experience to guide him.

Encouraging Men in Spiritual Matters

The source of a man's core identity is Christ. We want to be well-rounded men, rooted in Christ and growing in life. While we want to encourage spiritual sons in practical ways, nothing is more important than encouraging him in spiritual matters.

> *Christianity is not about behavior modification; it's about heart transformation.*

Early on, you'll want to consider where your spiritual son is on his own spiritual journey. Your role is not to be his pastor or his savior, but rather to guide him in the truth with the heart of a father.

At the end of the day, it is his responsibility to strive for spiritual growth. Any amount of pressure, obligation, or rules from you will not grow his spiritual faith.

The reason is simple: Christianity is not about behavior modification; it's about heart transformation.

If you have started meeting with a young man who doesn't know Christ, ask a lot of open-ended questions and look for opportunities to share your own beliefs and practices.

Be ready to answer any questions from him—but if you don't know the answer, don't fake it. Instead, tell him, "That's a great question and I'm not really sure what the right answer is. Let me do a little research and come back to you on that." And then, do the research! Ask your pastor or your small group how they would answer that question, and then be sure to follow up in your next meeting or phone call.

But if it's clear that the man you're meeting with is a professing Christian, then once you've built some rapport be direct in encouraging him to practice these three (at minimum) spiritual disciplines:

Prayer

Plenty of Christian men struggle to find time to pray or don't feel like they even know *how* to pray. If even the disciples asked Jesus how to pray, we can assume a spiritual son have questions or hesitations too.

If he expresses that he struggles with prayer, identify with him in that struggle. Even just letting him know that it's okay if he struggles is a first step toward a richer prayer life.

You might suggest that he starts small, praying over meals and before bed. Later, make suggestions that you have found helpful—maybe a book of prayers you like, or a method for journaling your prayers. And above all, *pray with him.*

You might also try this: at the end of every meeting, open up a text message and then share prayer requests with each other verbally. As each request is shared, type it into the text message. Hit Send before you leave the table. Now you each have a list of your prayer requests for the other and you can follow up between meetings. (Note: if one of his requests is highly personal and confidential, you may want to write it in your journal instead, as it's easier for someone else to see a text.)

Bible Reading

Christians rest on the Word. But as with prayer, when it comes to Bible reading, we often find it difficult to know where to begin—or jump back in after a long break. If a spiritual son hasn't read the Bible ever or in a while, remove that hurdle by encouraging him to start in a specific book.

> *The best way to encourage a younger man to spend time in Scripture consistently is to be in it yourself.*

You can make suggestions for best practices in reading the Bible diligently, but you should encourage this habit, not insist upon it. Guilt doesn't change people; love and grace do.

Instead, think about how you might participate with him in a Bible reading plan and talk about it when you meet. Or you may want to start with a short workbook or book that helps men apply the Bible to their lives. But you don't need to turn your meetings into Bible studies at the expense of getting to know each other and talking about real, day-to-day-life things. There are plenty of opportunities for that in small groups and Sunday School classes.

The best way to encourage a younger man to spend time in Scripture consistently is to be in it yourself. As you're faithful in that area of your own life, you will frequently find you are able to recall a pertinent passage when you are discussing a problem or issue together. Bring your Bible to meetings, and don't be bashful about referencing a passage as the occasion warrants.

Demonstrate how powerful God's word is in your life—that it is truly "living and active, sharper than any two-edged sword, piercing to the division of soul and of spirit, of joints and of marrow, and discerning the thoughts and intentions of the heart" (Hebrews 4:12).

Church Involvement

Men of all ages are typically less active and less diligent in their local church attendance than other groups. In many local churches, it's not uncommon to see a man's wife and kids there every week, only for him to show up periodically and reluctantly.

Your spiritual son may not be of this mindset, but if he is, help him see the value of local church engagement by modeling it for him. Encourage him to check out an upcoming opportunity to meet people and get more involved, like a couples' small group or a men's barbeque. If he doesn't currently have a local church home, invite him to come and sit with you at your weekend service, or offer to visit a local church of his choice with him.

Active participation in the local body of believers and a desire to serve and give back is a sign of spiritual maturity. Along these lines, tithing habits can also be raised at the appropriate time in conversations with your son. Giving joyfully is something we should encourage and model.

A note of caution: a small percentage of men need guidance in balancing local church involvement with other priorities. If your spiritual son has crammed his schedule with so many ministry-related commitments that he doesn't have time or energy for things like personal devotions or eating dinner with his children, encourage him to take inventory of his priorities. He may need your advice on how best to dial back his commitments. Remind him that if we spread ourselves too thin doing *good* things that other people could do, then we won't have space for the *best* things that only *we* can do.

A Spiritual Father and Son Story –
Chapter Ten: Sean Gets a Promotion

Sean was practically bouncing in his seat when Frank arrived for their regular meeting.

"Okay," Frank said. "Spill it."

"I got a promotion! And a raise!" Sean was beaming.

Frank knew this was a big deal. When they had first started meeting, Sean had been frustrated in his job. He had spent several meetings complaining about his job, his boss, his coworkers, and even the desk he had to work at. Frank had been patient and encouraging, and he had slowly seen Sean's attitude change.

When a job opened in another department that would be a vertical move for Sean, Frank had encouraged him to apply for it. They had talked through the interview process, and Frank had sent him some articles from business sites he thought would be helpful.

"Sean, I am so unbelievably proud of you," Frank said. And he found that he had not felt this good about another man's accomplishments since his own son, an aspiring journalist, had been published in a major magazine for the first time.

Later that week, he wrote a note to Sean congratulating him once again. He had written several notes to Sean over the months they had been meeting, and Sean had never mentioned them. But he didn't let that deter him.

A couple of weeks later, they met for lunch at a restaurant. As Sean was sliding into the booth, his notebook fell onto the floor, and a stack of cards fell out. As he picked them up sheepishly, Frank realized they were all the notes he had sent Sean.

Sean followed Frank's gaze and said, "I've saved every note you've ever written me. When I'm feeling down sometimes, I pull them out and read through them."

Takeaways

- Just as God dotes on his children as a loving Father, young men need spiritual fathers who provide regular encouragement.

- Encouragement should be vocal, liberal, and authentic.

- Praise your spiritual son directly when you notice growth.

- Speak highly of him in front of other people.

- Use milestones—good and bad—as an opportunity to show encouragement above and beyond what you would during normal conversation.

- Accountability is a two-way street. Encourage him to be accountable by building trust and modeling shared accountability.

- Encourage him to be mature in his life and faith.

- Guide him in practical ways related to family life, health, home repair, work, and finances.

- Encourage him in his spiritual walk to have disciplines of prayer, Bible reading, and church involvement.

- Remember: Any amount of pressure, obligation, or rules from you will not grow his spiritual faith. Christianity is not about behavior modification; it's about heart transformation.

Discussion

1) If you grew up with a father, did he lean toward critique or encouragement? How did that impact you?

2) In what areas in your life did you need the most encouragement in your 20s and 30s?

3) What is an area where you feel well equipped to encourage a spiritual son in a more tangible way? (It could be budgeting, cooking healthy meals, home repairs, parenting a teenager, Bible reading, etc.)

4) What are some ways in which you need encouragement in your own spiritual walk?

Special Note

With two chapters left in this study, you should be starting a serious discussion with your small group about where you are on making a decision to become a spiritual father. Continue to pray about the opportunity and keep considering the young men on the list you've created. If you have more than one man on your list at this point, arrange them in order of priority, and continue to pray for God's guidance and blessing as you proceed.

Prayer

Take a few minutes and share prayer requests around the group in the following areas: family, work, social, and personal.

Pray that the Lord would help you feel the encouragement of the Holy Spirit in your own spiritual disciplines, and that you can convey that to a spiritual son when the time is right.

Notes

CONFRONTING SIN

Selfishness, sexual immorality, substance abuse, workaholic behaviors—there are seemingly endless ways for a man to swerve off the path. Anytime we notice a pattern of sin beginning in the life of someone we care about, it requires an incredible amount of courage and grace to confront it. If you find yourself in this situation with your spiritual son, we want to provide you with some helpful strategies.

You should never be lying in wait for a moment to pounce on the slightest instance of sin or brokenness. Rather, you want to create an environment where he feels free and safe to come to you with his struggles. This chapter is intended to help you confront a destructive *pattern* of sin in his life—in a way that honors your relationship and God.

Law Never Changes a Man

First, be sure that you understand this biblical truth: men do not change as the result of threat or judgment.

The Law never changes a man. Paul is clear about this—God's standards are holy and just, but for sinners, they serve as a mirror to reveal our inherent brokenness (see Romans 7:7). We stand before God's law—like a mirror—naked and exposed. Our shame is obvious when the Law is the standard.

> *Using the Law to bring about change is like using an x-ray to heal a broken bone. The scan reveals the fracture, but it can do nothing to heal the break.*

Using the Law to bring about change is like using an x-ray scan to heal a broken bone. The scan reveals the fracture, but it can do nothing to heal the break. So, it is with the Law. It reveals the problem, but it changes nothing once revealed.

Consider the Pharisees. They relied on the Law as a demonstration of change, shaming those who didn't fulfil the Law as well as they did. But all the while, they ignored their *own* shortcomings and pursued a false holiness on their own terms, often through ego.

Declaring rules and barking commands does not produce fruit, and yet, like the Pharisees, so many earthly fathers resort to this method.

If you want to help a spiritual son change and grow, there's a better way.

Love + Grace = Change

It is a curious thing that we often forget to treat others how we wish to be treated (see Matthew 7:12). When we mess up, we don't want to be confronted with an attitude of harsh judgment. We don't want to be shamed, ostracized, or rejected.

God deals with our sin very differently than this. He knows our every weakness and asks only that we come broken to the cross. While Jesus didn't come to remove the mirror, so to speak (see Matthew 5:17), He did provide the final cure of forgiveness. And instead of receiving punishment, we receive the Holy Spirit into our hearts to cry Abba Father.

This has huge implications for us as spiritual fathers. The more compassion, love, and grace you can show a man who is caught in a pattern of sin, the better—even when he is hard to love.

Help your spiritual son focus not on guilt and shame, but rather on the freedom we have to confess our sins to each other and be vulnerable about our struggles. Because of Christ, we can share our brokenness without shame.

We add *nothing* to the work of Christ for our salvation. You can help a spiritual son grasp and rest in this incredible grace, as you demonstrate it in love. Only then will he experience real change.

Freedom from Outcomes

Before you go to someone to confront their sin, you must prepare your heart, especially when it's someone you're discipling.

The truth is you have no power to convict your spiritual son of their sin. That's God's role. Take your lead in this area from 2 Timothy 2:24-26:

> *The Lord's servant must not be quarrelsome but kind to everyone, able to teach, patiently enduring evil, correcting his opponents with gentleness.* God may perhaps grant them repentance *leading to a knowledge of the truth, and they may come to their senses and escape from the snare of the devil, after being captured by him to do his will.* (emphasis added)

It may be painful, but you must relinquish the outcomes. You are not the Lord, and no matter how perfect your words are, you don't grant repentance. God does. *Your* role is to be a fatherly voice, a gentle reminder—or even a strong reminder—of the wages of sin.

If a spiritual son is choosing to pursue a ruinous path, you are not responsible for his sin. You can't make him heed your advice or even be honest about his choices. It can hard to accept this when it's someone you care about, but the more you reflect on your own limitations, the more effective you will be if you must confront sin.

A Biblical Strategy

If you've decided that a destructive pattern of behavior needs to be addressed, here are steps we recommend you prayerfully take.

Start with Evidence

You cannot confront sin based on impressions or suspicions. If you have nothing more than a rumor or inkling that something is off, then you need to collect more information. Often, the best way to do this is by asking him directly:

> *How are things going with Hayley? I know you've talked about struggles in your marriage, but I'm getting a strong sense that maybe you're thinking of making a drastic mistake. Is there something going on we should talk about?*

If you have been journaling your conversations, over time you may see a pattern emerge that appears to be dangerous, such as consistently describing his children as burdensome, changing key details of stories, or repeatedly mentioning a female coworker in more favorable terms than his wife.

For example, you've noted in your journal several times the amount of drinking he does. In a sense, this is a form of evidence, and at this point, you should feel like you can raise the issue with your spiritual son, in love:

> *I've noticed over the last year that you seem to be drinking more and more. I feel like I need to bring this up as someone who cares about you. Sometimes it can be hard to recognize that it's becoming a problem because it's so culturally and socially accepted. But it can quickly shift. I've seen alcohol ruin a lot of lives over the years, so I just want to say please be careful. If you want to talk about this, I'm here for you.*

Without evidence, you have nothing to confront or raise with a spiritual son— only open questions to ask. But once you've confirmed that your concerns are warranted, the loving thing to do is bring them into the light.

Seek Wise Counsel

If you've become concerned about something serious in your spiritual son's life, you need to seek out wise counsel.

For some issues, your small group may be a good place to start. But confidentiality is still important in these situations. Each person should commit to absolute confidentiality among you (in the absence of behavior that is criminal or abusive).

If you can reach out to someone who has no connection to your spiritual son at all, that may be ideal. An older pastor or other Christian leader who lives in another city is a great example.

Whomever you go to for counsel, lean on his experience and listen to his advice. Importantly, he can also call you out if you're fixating on the wrong issues.

Raise the Issue Gently (At First)

This point needs to be repeated: Raise the issue gently.

Paul reminds the Galatians of this as well when he writes, "Brothers, if anyone is caught in any transgression, you who are spiritual should restore him in a spirit of gentleness" (Galatians 6:1a).

It is important that you identify with what's going on in his heart. This is easier, of course, if you have struggled with these same issues in your past; but even if you haven't, you can still relate to the pressure he is under. You need to pursue things softly:

> *I want to raise a sensitive matter. Let me say first that I can relate to what you're going through. But because you mean a lot to me, I have to bring something up with you in private.*

Watch your body language. Lean in and make sure to not cross your arms. Keep your face soft and neutral and avoid any tone of sternness in your voice. Reinforce that you are not sitting in judgment or feeling disappointed—that you identify and relate to what he's going through.

Above all, let him know that you are there for him. The more you can stress both grace and your desire for honesty, the better.

> *"Brothers, if anyone is caught in any transgression, you who are spiritual should restore him in a spirit of gentleness.*
> *(Galatians 6:1a)*

Bring An Ally

In rare cases, an intervention may be needed, meaning you involve another person in the discussion. Jesus gives us the pattern here when He says that the second round of confrontation involves bringing someone else in (see Matthew 18:16).

You must be very careful here. You don't want your spiritual son to feel like things are piling up on him, or that you are bringing shame or judgment.

But if there is another man whom 1) you can trust, and 2) you know also cares deeply about your spiritual son and is willing to pursue him in love, then approaching him together is a good idea. This is especially true with something that can be pernicious, such as substance abuse, pornography addiction, or an extramarital affair.

Leave the Door Open

While a spiritual son *may* hear you and be willing to be vulnerable with you in the moment, this is not always the case. Often, one's natural response to confrontation is a desire to escape. As a result, he may react in one of two toxic ways: denial or anger.

> *Leave the door open to hard conversations and an ongoing relationship.*

Denial when confronted with one's sin is when a man responds with, "I'm fine," or, "You don't know what you're talking about," or, "it's not a big deal." It's refusing to look into the mirror of God's Law. In cases of denial, having more than one voice of reason can often help. But if he refuses to see or admit the problem, it can be frustrating to try and continue the conversation.

You may be taken by surprise if met with an angry response. If you are, be careful not to lose your temper in return. Remember: his anger is not really aimed at you; it's a result of shame or his desire to continue in his sin. Rather than take responsibility for his behavior, he chooses to blame you for raising the point. But stick to the point: *I believe your behavior is self-destructive.*

Regardless of his reaction, be sure to stress that you are always open and willing to talk. He may see your confrontation as a rejection of him as a person. Be sure to communicate that this is not the case—that you care about him and will be there for him no matter what. Leave the door open to hard conversations and an ongoing relationship.

Restore Without Judgment

Once you have left the door open, you must be mentally and spiritually prepared for him to eventually walk back through it. Believe it or not, this can be difficult. If he expressed a lot of anger or blame toward you, his defenses may have hurt you. Talk about these feelings with your small group. Pray for a spirit of forgiveness, and then let your small group and the Holy Spirit heal your hurt feelings so you can love your spiritual son well.

In the Parable of the Prodigal Son (see Luke 15), the father's response to the return of his wayward son is a good model for us. Rather than rehashing his son's sin, he rushed to embrace him, even as his son wore the rags of his broken life.

> *"But the father said to his servants, 'Bring quickly the best robe, and put it on him, and put a ring on his hand, and shoes on his feet. And bring the fattened calf and kill it, and let us eat and celebrate. For this my son was dead, and is alive again; he was lost, and is found.' And they began to celebrate." (Luke 15:22-24)*

When Confrontation Leads to Division

We are all sinners, each of us in need of grace. We are not permitted to cut off a repentant believer because of his sin. Jesus is clear on this—we are to forgive all things just as our heavenly Father has forgiven us all things (see Matthew 6:14-15). And when the apostles ask Him how many times they must forgive, suggesting a generous number—"How about we forgive seven times?"—Jesus' answer is categorical— "You should forgive seventy times seven,"—which is a Jewish way of saying forgive to infinity (see Matthew 18:21-22).

In other words, Jesus does not allow us to keep a count of how many times or how badly someone has screwed up, cutting them off when it's too much. If there is remorse and repentance, then we should always seek a restoration of relationship, in grace.

There are times in the Bible, however, when sin does lead to a ruptured relationship. So how do we reconcile that?

In each case where sin leads to a rupture in a relationship, the situation involves a willful and purposeful choice to continue in a pattern of sin. For instance, in 1 Corinthians 5, Paul references throwing out a member of the church for sexual sin. The man in question isn't just sinning—he is telling everyone that he has the freedom to do so because of God's grace. Without any remorse or guilt, he is perverting the gospel.

There may come a time when we are confronted with a similar raw situation—a spiritual son is sinning, they have no regret, and they are not willing to hear from anyone who tells them to reconsider their ways.

If this happens to you, it is important to make it clear what you are seeing:

> *I know you're struggling, and maybe you find this is a way to sort of numb that pain. I've had those impulses too at certain times in my life. But I'm concerned that your heart seems eager to sin.*

In the rare event that he wants nothing to do with repentance, then it is appropriate for you to get some space. That said, we encourage you to stay in his life in some way if possible.

Sometimes, a man who is willfully sinning and pursuing self-destruction will start to avoid *you*. As we have said, you need to be ready to relinquish the outcome. If he walks away, you have done what you've been called to do. Continue to pray for him, without losing hope.

A Spiritual Father and Son Story –
Chapter Eleven: Sean Screws Up

To Frank, the last few conversations with Sean had felt off—a little shallow and short, compared to their usual rhythms.

He knew Sean had been feeling a little frustrated in his marriage recently. Although he hadn't gone into detail, he had mentioned on a few occasions that he and his wife were both exhausted all the time from work and kids, and there just wasn't any sense of intimacy between them over the last couple of months— emotionally or physically.

He had also casually mentioned a new female colleague a couple of times, remarking on her sense of humor.

Still, when Frank had gently prodded, Sean assured him everything was fine. Knowing a gut feeling wasn't exactly ironclad evidence that something more was wrong, Frank decided to pray for him until their next meeting, which was two days away. He asked Sean if he could come to his office for lunch instead of their usual restaurant, so they'd have more privacy.

During the first 15 minutes of their time together, as they made *unusually small* talk, Frank noticed that Sean kept receiving texts. He'd glance down, but instead of mentioning it or replying, Sean looked increasingly tense, eventually just silenced his phone and turned it facedown. A red flag went up in Frank's mind. He decided to be more direct this time.

"Sean," he started, leaning in, "What's up with your phone? I could be way off base here, but it's too important to avoid asking. Is something going on that you're not telling me? You can tell me anything, you know."

Silence. Frank continued, "I'll take a guess, and forgive me if I'm wrong. But I know things have been rough recently at home, and in those times, it could be easier for a man's eyes to wander, or for his thoughts to go places they shouldn't. I just don't want you to get yourself in a position that compromises your marriage or your integrity."

After what felt like an eternity, Sean closed his eyes and took a deep breath. When he looked back up at Frank, he looked like he was holding back tears. Then it all came out in a rush.

He admitted that he had grown close to his new coworker. She was bright, funny, and shared many of the same interests as him. Although nothing physical had happened, he had thought about it once and immediately felt guilty.

But then a week ago, she had invited him out with a group of coworkers after work. He asked his wife if she minded if he went out for a little while with them, and she said that was okay. But when he got to the restaurant, there were no other coworkers there. It was just the two of them.

"I knew I should just leave, but I didn't," Sean said. "We got a table and ordered dinner, talking and learning more about each other. It was about halfway through dinner when it hit me." He paused. "I realized I was on a date."

He felt so guilty, he told Frank, that he had quickly paid and bolted from the restaurant. "I feel horrible. I can't even look my wife in the eyes. It's like I cheated on her!" The tears came then.

Frank was crushed to hear that his gut feeling had checked out, but also relieved that Sean wasn't hiding any longer. He looked Sean in the eye. "First of all, I want to tell you that I am proud of you for getting yourself out of that situation. That was the Holy Spirit prodding your conscience, and you listened. I also want to tell you that I love you, and I'm grateful that you opened up to me about this.

"You're absolutely right, though; in a way, it *is* like you cheated on your wife. You let your guard down and took the first steps toward an emotional affair. I get that your behavior at work toward this woman was probably innocent at first. But when you start looking forward to seeing a female coworker, talking with her, and joking around with her, recognize that you are on dangerous ground."

"I see that now—*clearly*," Sean said. "I should've never let it get this far." He sighed. "So, what do you think I should do now?"

Frank and Sean talked for another hour about next steps for Sean—steps that included telling his wife that his coworkers didn't show up for dinner, establishing firm boundaries with the woman he worked with, making an appointment with a marriage counselor, intentionally carving out time every single evening with his wife, and more.

It took some time, but things began to improve between Sean and his wife.

A few months later, as Frank was updating his group, one of the other spiritual fathers said, "You know, Frank. A long time ago I wrecked my first marriage by having an affair that started in a similar way. I wasn't as strong as Sean, and I didn't get out when I should have. But if I'd had a guy like you in my life, I think the outcome would have been much different, and my family would have been spared a lot of heartbreak."

Takeaways

- It takes an incredible amount of courage and grace to confront sin in the life of someone we love.

- Men do not change as the result of threat or judgment.

- The more compassion, love, and grace you can show a man who is caught in a pattern of sin, the better.

- Because of Christ, we can share our brokenness without shame.

- No matter how perfect your approach, you don't grant repentance. God does. Your role is to be a fatherly voice gently reminding him of the wages of sin.

- A biblical strategy for confronting a pattern of sin is to 1) start with evidence, 2) seek wise counsel, 3) raise the issue gently, 4) bring an ally, 5) leave the door open, and 6) restore without judgment.

- If a rupture in the relationship occurs, continue to pray for your spiritual son.

Discussion

1) Thinking about a time when someone confronted you in your sin, was it done well or in a way that brought shame and condemnation?

2) Who is someone you can go to for wise counsel if you need it?

3) Read through the Parable of the Prodigal Son in Luke 15 as a group. Who do you identify with most in this story—the son, the father, or the brother?

4) Are there any factors that could hinder your ability to confront a pattern of sin in a spiritual son's life, should the need arise?

Prayer

Take a few minutes and share prayer requests around the group in the following areas: family, work, social, and personal.

Pray for wisdom, gentleness, and courage to confront sin in a spiritual son if needed.

Share the name of the man you are considering inviting into this process and pray over him with your small group.

Notes

CHAPTER 12

WHEN A RELATIONSHIP ENDS

While the hope is that the relationship between a spiritual father and son will flourish and last, this may not always be the case.

If the discipleship relationship does need to conclude, how you end it is almost as important as how you start it. That's why this last chapter of the guidebook is devoted to equipping you to recognize the signs a relationship is ending, process it, and handle it well every step of the way.

Why Discipleship Relationships End

It's tempting to assume that all relationships should be permanent—especially in this age of social media. It is far too easy to feel like we're connected to those from our past without having any active, living relationship with them.

But a relationship that ends is not always a bad thing. Nor is it true that relationships end only when there is drama or frustration.

> *If the discipleship relationship does need to conclude, how you end it is almost as important as how you start it.*

Sometimes, yes, relationships end due to poor communication, loss of trust, or other serious issues. But sometimes priorities or circumstances simply shift.

This chapter will give you guidance on the best way to end the spiritual father-son relationship well, should you sense it needs to end.

There are various signs that this might be the case, which can be divided into three categories: 1) signs the relationship is ending naturally, 2) signs the relationship has run its course, or 3) signs the relationship has problems.

The Relationship Is Ending Naturally
Some relationships end naturally. Possible reasons include:

- A serious illness or other physical limitation that makes it impossible to continue.
- One person moving to a new city.
- A spiritual son focusing on a new discipleship relationship with someone else, such as his pastor.

In these cases, the relationship comes to an end because of changing circumstances. Nothing was wrong; in a different situation, the relationship would have continued. But for practical reasons, it is impossible to continue with the level of closeness inherent to the spiritual father-son relationship.

That said, it doesn't mean the friendship has to end altogether. In the Bible, we see that Paul was like a father to Timothy, and the two were side by side in ministry for years. But later, they had to separate for the sake of ministry. Although the relationship looked different, they maintained their connection over distance, and Paul never lost sight of his role in Timothy's life as a spiritual father and brother in Christ.

The Relationship Has Run Its Course

It is acceptable to disciple a young man for a season. The ideal, of course, is a lifelong relationship that ebbs and flows with the years as you both grow together. But in a few instances, it is natural for the relationship to evolve into something new. Reasons for these changes include:

- You fathered him through a specific season of life.
- You fathered him through a crisis.
- Your spiritual son has matured over time to the point where *he* is now ready to guide a man who is farther behind him on his journey.

It can be a delicate balance between encouraging a man to stay committed to good things that are helping him grow, and not pressuring him if he feels ready for a change.

Perhaps the relationship initially formed out of a grief group, college ministry, or addiction recovery program. There was no barrier or conflict that caused the relationship to end prematurely. Instead, the father-son relationship was for a particular season or purpose.

However, if possible, try to define a new path together versus ending the relationship entirely.

For example, if the man you've been discipling has a new baby and expresses that he needs to meet less frequently, it is not unreasonable to do that. Discuss what would work well for him and ask how you can support him in this new season.

It can be a delicate balance between encouraging a man to stay committed to good things that are helping him grow, and not pressuring him if he feels ready for a change.

But hear this: If your spiritual son feels like your relationship has run its course, you should never take it as a personal slight or rejection.

The Relationship Has Problems

Some spiritual father-son relationships simply don't work. The problems can be relatively benign or more serious:

- Personality differences or conflicting communication styles
- Perpetual lying or other toxic behaviors
- Consistent resistance to meeting or connecting in any meaningful way

In certain cases, the need to end the relationship is clear. If a spiritual son is lying or manipulating, regularly standing you up, or flagrantly violating your boundaries, then the need to walk away eventually becomes clear.

The key word here is "eventually." It is important that you refrain from rushing into the decision quickly—especially when you are feeling angry or disappointed. Seek counsel from your small group, a pastor, mentor, or trusted friend who can help guide you to your right next step.

But sometimes relationships fail no matter how much we strive to make them work.

The Worst Thing You Can Do

By far the worst thing you can do is end things with your spiritual son without clear communication and love.

A spiritual father-son relationship should never end with a whimper—where the father drags it out slowly, misses meetings, and slacks on communication, before finally stopping in a way that leaves both men unsure of where things stand.

> *A father-son relationship should never end with a whimper.*

This passive approach can be damaging to a spiritual son's sense of security, trust in others, and faith—especially if he has father wounds.

And if you neglect to communicate the situation clearly to your spiritual son, you are leaving it up to his imagination to figure out what went wrong—where he went wrong. At best, he may assume you simply lost interest. At worst, the imagination of someone who feels rejected turns into a nightmare.

So why would any spiritual father allow this to happen? Here are some things that leave us vulnerable to this dreaded scenario:

- Slacking on our commitment to prayer and journaling
- Doing less than the minimum 1-2-3 Method of communication
- Missing meetings due to vacation, work, holiday seasons, or general busyness
- Struggling to find things to discuss or process together

- Lacking support from other spiritual fathers
- Being new to discipling someone else

If you sense that what once was a strong, growing connection has begun to slow or fade, prayerfully consider what changes you might need to make before calling it quits.

How to End Things Well

If you've made the tough decision to end the relationship, for whatever reason, you need to take intentional steps to do it as well as you can.

1. Prepare your words.

Make sure you know what you are going to say before you start the conversation. Do not bring it up until you are ready—and you are not ready until you have the words rehearsed. It may even be helpful to write them out first and practice, or to share it with another spiritual father or your small group.

2. Do it in person.

There is rarely an excuse for not looking your spiritual son in the eye while telling him you need to end the relationship. Some spiritual fathers struggle with the fear of letting their son down. But never compound the situation by ending the relationship through another form of communication, such as calling or texting.

> *Never compound the situation by ending the relationship through a less personal form of communication, such as calling or texting.*

In the rare event that something does make it impossible to meet in person, you may need to end it with a phone call. But this should always be the absolute last resort.

3. You do not have to explain everything.

If you are worried about letting your spiritual son down, you may be tempted to go into great detail to explain why you're ending things. Try to avoid this. Often, the more you over-explain, the more it sounds like an excuse.

For example, if you are having struggles with your health, as well as stress at home, and your work is ramping up to the point that you simply cannot pull it all off—don't feel as if you must lay all of it out in detail. And if there's something you prefer to keep private, that's within your rights to do so.

4. But you *do* need to explain *some* things.

While you don't need to go into all the details, you should provide—clearly—some of the reasons why you need to end the relationship.

This, of course, may be harder if you must end things because of his actions or poor reception to the discipleship process. But even then, it will give your spiritual son closure if you let him know why you are choosing to step away.

5. Affirm your love.

In the end, make sure you let him know that you love him and only good things for him. Even in hard cases where the relationship is strained, send him away in peace, so much as it depends on you.

6. Set a firm end date.

Communicate a firm, but somewhat future, end date—if at all possible. This doesn't work for every situation, of course, but the less sudden the break, the better.

No matter when the end date is, though, it should be clearly articulated to your spiritual son.

One note: If your spiritual son is moving out of town, you may be able to maintain a relationship via video or phone calls. But the best arrangement for discipleship is face to face and shoulder to shoulder. Encourage him to pursue Christian friendships in his new city, while also looking for someone local who could spiritually invest in him. This might take a while, but you can walk with him through the process, and hopefully you will remain friends for a lifetime.

7. Leave the door open.

As discussed in the previous chapter, it may be good to leave the door open for you to resume the relationship in the future. If you are willing—and if you are clear about what would need to change *first*—then let your spiritual son know that you'd like to start again if the Lord wills it.

In cases where you need to walk away from a toxic situation, pray that this step of leaving the door open someday bears fruit.

8. Be ready to grieve.

It can be difficult if someone you have invested time, energy, and encouragement into *cannot* or *does not* stay in relationship with you. Like with any close friendship that ends, feeling sad or discouraged is natural.

And if the relationship was hard or riddled with conflict and you had to take steps to end it, you may also feel guilt that can be further compounded by a sense of relief. Again, it's so important to talk with other spiritual fathers who can help you process these feelings.

Regardless of who ends the relationship, though, we want you to feel free of any guilt or feelings of failure—even if you made some mistakes along the way.

If you have journaled and prayed and counseled with others during your time as his spiritual father, recognize that *nothing has been in vain. This relationship was a part of his spiritual journey, and yours.*

Take some time to process this experience and any lessons you have learned. Then, when you are ready, prayerfully look around—most likely, God has another young man He has prepared for you to invest in with the heart of a father.

A Spiritual Father and Son Story –
Chapter Twelve: When a Relationship Ends

Frank was in a small group with two other spiritual fathers: Phil and Howard. They met once a month for coffee and texted with each other regularly.

While Frank's relationship with Sean was flourishing, Phil's relationship with his spiritual son Matt was not. Because of some work issues, Phil had struggled to connect with Matt from the start. Their schedules didn't match up well and they each had canceled meetings at the last minute. A couple of months in, they finally got their scheduling kinks worked out, but then other tensions arose.

Once they got to know each other better, Matt started fluctuating between going incommunicado and overwhelming Phil with texts and calls—at all hours of the night. He would become angry when Phil set boundaries on times that he could reach him. Frank and Howard encouraged Phil to set some clearer expectations, but even when he did, the pattern continued. All the while, both Matt and Phil had become increasingly frustrated.

Phil shared with the guys that at their last meeting, Matt had told Phil he wasn't there for him when he needed him. When Phil had tried to explain that he had responsibilities at work and to his family that he also had to honor, Matt had stormed out of their meeting.

Their calls and texts since then had been strained at best. Phil was about to enter another busy season at work, and while he felt like they could maintain at least a monthly face-to-face meeting and weekly contacts via text and phone calls— at appropriate hours—he sensed that Matt would regard any reduction in his availability as rejection.

Frank and Howard listened until Phil was finished, and then they prayed for wisdom together. Before they left, they agreed to pray separately for one week about the situation and then meet again.

One week came and went, and they all prayed daily like they had committed to doing. In addition, Phil read back through his journal. When they met up over lunch, they were all in agreement that Phil would probably never be a good fit for Matt, and that he needed to end the relationship before it became more toxic, bringing neither man any benefit nor growth. Frank and Howard let Phil think through and practice what he would say to Matt.

When Phil met with Matt to discuss his decision, Frank actually went and sat in the coffee shop at a different table. Just like he'd practiced, Phil was kind and straightforward with Matt. Without criticizing him, he told him that he didn't think he could meet Matt's expectations and that it didn't seem like it made sense to continue spending time together. Surprisingly, Matt handled it well and said he understood. He surprised Phil by apologizing for not honoring his boundaries and said he had nevertheless gotten something from the time they'd spent hanging out. They shook hands and left on a positive note.

Frank and Phil sat in the coffee shop afterward to process it. Frank affirmed Phil's handling of the situation, and they prayed together.

Phil continued to meet with Frank and Howard each month, discussing his missteps with Matt and what he'd learned from the experience. After a few months, he sensed that he was ready to try again, and he showed up to their next meeting with a list of a few young men to pray about investing in.

Takeaways

- Your relationship as a spiritual father and son may come to an end. Make sure it ends well.

- Some relationships end due to circumstances: a move, a better fit with another spiritual father, or an illness that prevents you from meeting. This is not your fault.

- Some relationships end because they have run their course. Celebrate the benefits of the relationship to that point, and then adjust as necessary for a new season.

- Some relationships end because there are persistent problems. And they fail no matter how much we strive to make them work.

- No matter what, don't just let the relationship peter out. Bring it to an intentional end.

- It may take several conversations, but be clear, honest, and affirming—and meet face to face. Set clear expectations with a firm ending date.

- Be prepared to grieve the ending of the relationship. Talk through those feelings with some men who are close to you, preferably other spiritual fathers.

- Prayerfully consider what your next steps should be, and who else God may be calling you to invest in.

Discussion

1) What lessons have you learned from ending relationships in the past?

2) Describe a time when someone ended a relationship with you. Did they do it well, and if not, how?

3) In the section The Worst Thing You Can Do, which items in the bulleted list are you particularly vulnerable to?

4) How has this experience impacted your own spiritual journey so far?

Congratulations!

You have completed the spiritual fathers small group together! Take some time to discuss the highlights of what you've learned about being a spiritual father and about each other.

Closing Discussion

1) What are the most important lessons you've learned from this study?

2) Are you planning to become a spiritual father? Why or why not?

3) If you are planning to become a spiritual father, who is the young man you have in mind to invest in?

4) What is your timeline for getting started?

5) How will your small group continue to support each other as spiritual fathers?

Next Steps Conversation

Our prayer is that by reading this book with your small group, you have learned more about why young men are struggling, the incredible opportunity that exists to help young men grow and the potential you have to make a huge difference by investing in the life of a young man as a spiritual father.

So, what's next?

Man in the Mirror has created four quarterly journal sets--one for you and one for your spiritual son--to guide your conversations together. The journals are designed to be done in sequence, helping you build a meaningful relationship over time.

1. **Known** – 13 questions to facilitate conversations around the story and background of your lives.

2. **Loved** – This journal facilitates conversations exploring the key relationships in a man's life.

3. **Trinity** – The most important relationship of all: relating to God as Father, Son, and Spirit.

4. **Vision** – Based on the conversations prompted by the first three journals, help your spiritual son develop a practical plan for personal growth moving forward.

You can purchase these journals individually or all together on the Man in the Mirror website.

Take the Next Step with a Spiritual Son:

1. Scan the QR code below

2. Make your initial journal purchase decision (1 set at a time or all 4 sets at once.)

3. Purchase and receive your spiritual father journal set/sets.

4. Review and follow the outline in chapter 3 for engaging with a potential spiritual son.

Prayer

Take a few minutes and share prayer requests around the group in the following areas: family, work, social, and personal.

Pray for your first interactions with a potential spiritual son—that God would bless you in your efforts and help you develop a strong bond in the months ahead as a spiritual father and son.

Notes

ACKNOWLEDGEMENTS

ACKNOWLEDGEMENTS

Like all books, this one took a team effort to create. We'd like to thank: Dale Redder for his project management oversight of this book and the entire spiritual fathers rollout; Jeremy Schurke for his insights and vision for the initiative and for this book; Wayne Morgret for his suggestions and input, particularly on the Emotions chapter; and Jamie Turco for her editing and input to make this book excellent.

This project was initially rolled out in seven pilot cities across the country under the leadership of Man in the Mirror Area Directors Larry Niggli, Greg English, Gary Canupp, Nate Flynn, Dan Hindman, Phil Elmore, Mark Somers, and Peter Hone. The feedback from this group was instrumental in finetuning and focusing the book.

The second edition, including the title change and many helpful edits and updates, was overseen by Scott Mawdesley, program director of the spiritual fathers initiative.

We'd also like to thank our entire staff of Area Directors for working tirelessly around the country to help churches build a culture of discipleship.

And to all the spiritual fathers who have come before and are yet to come we pray that you will keep investing in the lives of men behind you on their journey, guiding them towards a life of reflecting honestly, pursuing God wholeheartedly, and living vibrantly.

APPENDICES:
BEST PRACTICES

I. THE EMOTIONS WHEEL

One of the most successful tools developed to help men identify underlying emotions is the emotions wheel. By asking good questions, you can guide a spiritual son through the use of this emotions wheel to identify his emotions.

As you can see below, the emotions wheel gives a man a way to put words to what he is feeling by giving him both a process and a vocabulary. Starting from the middle and working his way out, your spiritual son can become more precise in expressing his emotions.

Some of the benefits of using the emotions wheel are:

Trust: When someone shares their emotions with another, it creates an environment of trust and openness.

Clarity: Walking around with a mind full of confusion and uncertainty would make anyone feel sad, mad, or overwhelmed. This is especially true for young men who want to understand themselves or a stressful situation but don't know where to start. With the emotions wheel, your spiritual son can browse the various emotions and pinpoint the specific ones he is experiencing.

Communication: Being able to express his emotions accurately and calmly is a tool that will help a spiritual son in every key relationship in his life.

Self-Awareness: Understanding his emotions will help a man address the root of a problem or issue, rather than the behavioral response. It helps him focus on the heart issues involved and not just the external behavior.

Before You Use the Emotions Wheel

Take some time to familiarize yourself with the wheel. Practice using it with your wife, friends, and small group members. You may find it is an extremely helpful tool for you!

Don't pull the emotions wheel out the first time your spiritual son expresses a vague emotion. Yes, the emotions wheel can help you deepen your relationship, but trust must already exist before you use it.

Finally, it is a tool to use only when your spiritual son needs it. For instance, if you meet several times and notice that he is experiencing intense emotions but is having difficulty expressing them clearly, mention that the next time you meet, you'd like to show him a tool that he might find helpful when he is trying to put words to his feelings. Bring the emotions wheel to the next meeting.

Using the Emotions Wheel

When you've determined it will be helpful, give your son the emotions wheel to look at. Give him a minute or so to look it over.[27]

Ask him, "Can you point to one of the emotions in the center of the wheel that best describes the emotion you are feeling about this topic?" Give him a few seconds to take it all in. Remember, this might be the first time anyone has ever asked him to identify an emotion.

When he picks an emotion that seems closest to how he feels, ask him to then go out a level to the emotions attached to it to see if there is a word that more precisely describes his emotion. And

---

[27] A printable color version of the emotions wheel is available at www.spiritualfathers.com

repeat this process again for the next level. Once he gets to the word that he thinks fits best (and there could be more than one), take some time to talk about the emotion and where it's coming from.

If he is struggling initially, let him look over the entire wheel first and pick a few words that might describe his emotions. Then spend time discussing them and try to bring clarity.

Remember: The goal is to have a more meaningful conversation. You are not there to be his therapist. You are there to give him tools to grow as a man, know himself better, and live a more successful and fulfilling life.

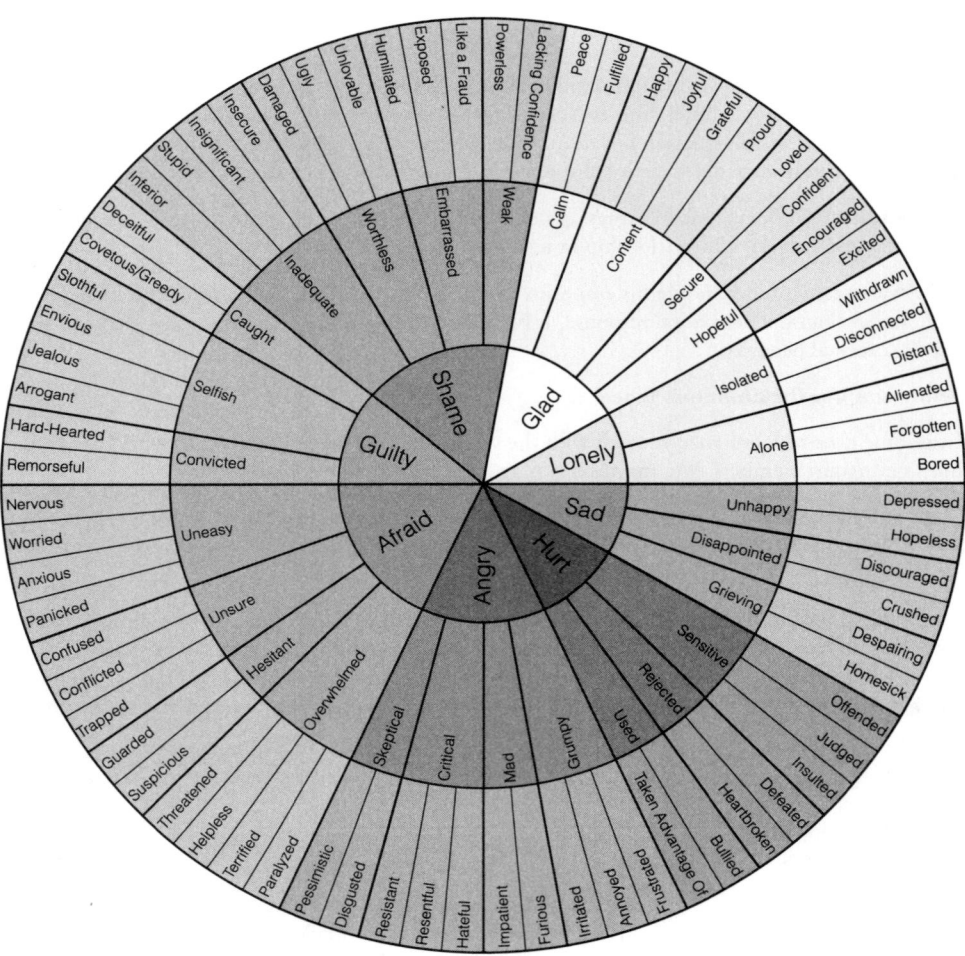

Feelings Wheel © 2015 K. Timothy Burkholder, MAC, LMHC, CSAT
ktburkholder@chariscounselingcenter.com

144

II. REMAIN A DISCIPLE

No matter how much you care and how skilled you are in your role as a spiritual father, it's vital to prioritize your own spiritual health and growth. Just as you would encourage the man you are meeting with to maintain basic spiritual disciplines; we want to encourage you to be faithful in these five areas:

1. **Remain Active in the Local Church**

   As Christians, we need the local church and a local family of believers in our journey as disciples of Jesus Christ (see Hebrews 10:25). It helps us stay connected to the regular teaching of the Word, the fellowship of the saints, opportunities to serve, and a place to invest your time, talent, and treasure. While you don't have to attend every event, potluck, Sunday School class, or elder meeting, being committed and consistently engaged in the life of the local church is a must.

2. **Remain in the Word**

   Based on our 30+ years of ministry experience, lasting transformation takes place within men who are regularly reading and applying God's word. Living and active, it produces growth and fruit in your life: "so shall my word be that goes out from my mouth; it shall not return to me empty, but it shall accomplish that which I purpose, and shall succeed in the thing for which I sent it" (Isaiah 55:11). And of course, the more consistently you are in the Scriptures, the more you'll sense the Holy Spirit's prompting when you need truth in conversations with your spiritual son.

3. **Remain in Prayer**

   As with the Word, so it is with prayer. How you pray, in what order, and at what time of day are non-essentials; what is essential is that you pray consistently. Prayer is so important that the Bible tells us that Jesus Christ Himself sits at the right hand of God interceding on our behalf (see Romans 8:34). Remain consistent in prayer and you will find your thoughts becoming more tuned to the voice of the Holy Spirit.

4. **Remain Connected to a Pastor or Spiritual Leader**

   We all need someone with greater maturity than us to be a listening ear—someone who will lift our arms when we're tired, correct us in love, and show us the grace of a shepherd. If you don't already have someone like this in your life, a good starting point may be your pastor or another leader in your local church. Ideally, you will have your own spiritual father—guiding you as you guide your spiritual son.

   Just as you need a spiritual father or mentor to help guide you, you need brothers to walk beside you. We suggest these men be other spiritual fathers so that you can support each other, discuss the challenges you are facing, and look for answers together in Scripture to the tough questions you may be asked. Try to meet with these guys at least monthly to discuss your spiritual father-son relationships and encourage each other.

*Note: In addition to Spiritual Fathering, Man in the Mirror has various resources to help you grow, including books, devotions, webinars, articles, and more! Visit **maninthemirror.org** to see how we can serve and support you as you seek to reflect honestly, pursue God wholeheartedly,and live vibrantly.*

III. JOURNAL THE RELATIONSHIP

It will be incredibly helpful over the course of a spiritual father-son relationship to keep a record of your journey. Man in the Mirror has a series of three-month prayer journals designed to walk you through the first year of being a spiritual father.

Keep your prayer journal close so that you can write in it...

1. Daily; as you pray for your spiritual son, perhaps at the end of your regular devotional time, write down the thoughts God brings to mind, specific prayers for your son, etc.

2. After every face-to-face meeting, jot some notes to remind you of the important points discussed, events coming up in his life, prayer requests, etc.

3. After a difficult or uplifting interaction, whether by phone, text, or in person.

4. When the Lord prompts you to write something down that pertains to your relationship, such as after a conversation with your spiritual fathers' small group.

Paul wrote, "Him we proclaim, warning everyone and teaching everyone with all wisdom, that we may present everyone mature in Christ. For this I toil, struggling with all his energy that he powerfully works within me" (Colossians 1:28-29).

This is our goal! Journaling is a great way for you to keep account of this progress toward maturity.

If you are wondering what to write about, here are some ideas:

- A log of the interactions you had during the week (phone, text, in person), with any thoughts about the interaction you might have.

- Specific prayers for your spiritual son. Note beside the prayer whether it is something he requested you pray for, or if it is your own prayer on his behalf.

- Problems he expressed with his marriage, children, work, parents, friends, finances, health, church, or other areas of his life. This is especially important if it's something you want to follow up with him about.

- A behavior or attitude that you noticed and want to encourage.

- A behavior or attitude that you noticed and might want to prayerfully address.

- Times where you have had difficulty communicating or connecting with him—and what you might've done to contribute.

- Any boundaries that you need to establish or reinforce.

- Possible future plans, including activities or meeting places.

- Goals.

Having a running dialogue with yourself about how things are going will help you be more effective and intentional. You may even want to conclude each year or quarter by going over your notes and prayers.

As the journey with your spiritual son unfolds, your journals will be of immense value to you. Through the prayers, thoughtfulness, and commitment captured, you will honor God, your calling, and your spiritual son.

IV. SHOULDER-TO-SHOULDER ACTIVITIES

We've seen this saying often, in various forms, and it rings true: *Women tend to bond face to face in shared conversation. Men tend to bond shoulder to shoulder in shared experiences and responsibilities.*

You may think that most of the impact you have will be in face-to-face conversations. And you will make an impact during these times, since talking about life, faith, and emotions is essential to the father-son relationship. But close relationships are best built through shared experiences.

Men do very well when they are shoulder to shoulder. Doing things together—whether it is recreational like playing a round of golf, task-oriented like a work project, or experiential like providing a ride to the airport—provides for informal conversations, shared memories, and even inside jokes that build a foundation for future interactions.

Here are some tips for incorporating shoulder-to-shoulder discipleship.

Do Something You Both Enjoy

Don't feel like you must do something because it's "what men do." All that matters is that you both enjoy it, whether it's physical labor outside, working out, sports, computer games, live music, darts or pool, etc. It may be tempting to overthink it initially, but it's simple—find a common interest and make a plan to do it.

Fun > Instruction

When you do invite him to go out for something fun, don't feel like you need to (or even should) talk about life and theology. Deeper topics may come up naturally—and feel free to delve in if your son starts the conversation. But it's not a time of instruction. Just enjoying each other's company is well worth the time invested.

When In Doubt, Do Something New

If you and your spiritual son don't have a lot of common interests, that's okay! Think of it as an opportunity to try something new. For example, if your son loves fishing, then gladly go fishing, even if it's not your first choice—or second or third. Part of taking an interest in someone else's life is being open to trying the things they enjoy.

Look for Opportunities

If your spiritual son often laments that his house needs some repairs, but he doesn't know how and you do, offer to come over and show him. Bring your tools (and your sense of humor). If he's often mentioned that he wished he had continued in Little League, go to a batting cage together. Pay attention in conversation, jot down notes and ideas in your journal, and take advantage of these opportunities to build a deeper relationship.

V. TAKE A SABBATICAL

When needed, it is perfectly good and wise to take a break from your spiritual father-son relationship for a brief season.

There are some specific times and triggers that may prompt you to take a short break:

- **Vacation:** If you are taking a vacation, particularly with your family, you should also take a vacation from your responsibilities as a spiritual father. A vacation is designed to give yourself time to rest and recharge—spiritually, mentally, and emotionally. In addition, we want you to give the loved ones you're with 100% of your attention. (By the way, this goes for your spiritual son's vacations, too!)

- **Work Challenges:** If you know you are coming into a particularly heavy season of work travel or projects, it may be good for you to communicate that and the need to take a planned break. This will keep you from seeming aloof or distracted and allow you to give the focus you need to the task at hand for a few weeks if necessary.

- **Spiritual Fatigue:** For all of us at times, life seems to require more energy than we have to give. If you start to recognize a growing sense of feeling overwhelmed or numb, honor it. That last thing you want to do is run out of the spiritual or emotional energy to care. Take a break for a few weeks! There is no benefit to either of you if you burn out. Use that time to rest, focus on your relationship with Christ, and pray for strength and renewal so that you can be more fully present for your family and your spiritual son.

Think of this as a sabbatical—a break with a purpose so that you can return stronger. Taking a sabbatical will also show your spiritual son the importance of taking care of himself.

When you feel like you need time to rest and be refreshed, first decide on a time frame. If you're going on a vacation, this will be obvious. But if not, we recommend a duration range of two weeks to two months. Anything longer should be avoided. Then communicate that to your son. Call it a sabbatical and make it clear that you are doing this for rest—and that you look forward to reconnecting with him when you return.

Feel free to still send him a text now and then, when appropriate. If you're traveling, for example, this could include a photo of a place you're visiting or some other interesting fact.

But the most important part is what happens afterward. When you return from a sabbatical, refreshed and spiritually renewed, return to your normal rhythms of communicating and hanging out with your spiritual son.

VI. FALSE STARTS

Sometimes, very early in the process, things will fizzle out. It's okay if things just don't work out. We call these "false starts."

But here are some questions to think or journal through, should that happen. These aren't designed to beat you up, but rather to help you in subsequent relationships.

Did I pray for the relationship?

If you prayed diligently for the relationship at the start, then you should take comfort in that. If you neglected prayer, then resolve to do better next time. Don't be too hard on yourself; it's an opportunity to grow increasingly faithful in what God is calling you to do. Continue to check in with yourself and stay committed to prayer.

How could I have done better?

New spiritual fathers are not immune to mistakes—even veteran spiritual fathers make mistakes. Areas to consider include:

- **Communication:** Was it regular? Was I as responsive as I should have been?

- **Encouragement:** Did I come across as judgmental? Did I celebrate victories or just comment on setbacks? Did I spur him on to be his best?

- **Reliability:** Did I do what I said I would when I said I would do it? Did I change or miss plans regularly?

After going through these questions, write out what you could do differently to help foster a sense of connection and build the relationship next time around.

Even if it was him who became distant, cold, or unreliable, you should still check in to see if you could do anything different next time.

What did I learn from this false start?

We are all men who live under God's grace, so we admit when we've made mistakes. But learning from those mistakes is crucial.

Maybe you learned what forms of communication work best for what situations. Maybe you realize you came on too strong too soon. Maybe you learned something about when you are or aren't at your best, such as lunch meetings being rushed due to your work schedule.

Use these realizations to make adjustments. Fathering is a skill, and you hone your skill by striving to improve.

X̄

SPIRITUAL FATHERS

MAN IN THE MIRROR